FIERCE *with* REALITY

An Anthology of
Literature on Aging

Margaret Cruikshank, Editor

REVISED EDITION

Acknowledgments on page vii are considered to be a part of this copyright page.

Cover Photo: Copyright © 2006 Nancy E. Randolph

Library of Congress Catalog Card No. 2006932189

Editor: Cruikshank, Margaret
Fierce with Reality
p. 352
1. Literary Collections-General
2.Psychology-Developmental - Adulthood & Aging
3. Family & Relationships-Aging - General
1. Title.

ISBN-13: 978-0-9788628-0-0
ISBN-10: 0-9788628-0-5

Printed in the United States of America

First North Star Press Edition: September 1995
First Just Write Books Edition: November 2006

Published by

JWB

Just Write Books
47 Main Street #3, Topsham, Maine 04086
207-729-3600 • www.jstwrite.com

"You need only claim the events of your life to make yourself yours. When you truly possess all you have been and done, which may take some time, you are fierce with reality. When at last age has assembled you together, will it not be easy to let it all go, lived, balanced, over?"

—Florida Scott-Maxwell
The Measure of My Days

The Old Poets of China

Wherever I am, the world comes after me.
It offers me its busyness. It does not believe
that I do not want it. Now I understand
why the old poets of China went so far and high
into the mountains, then crept into the pale mist.

Mary Oliver

Acknowledgments

Arte Publico Press, University of Houston, for two poems: Judith Ortiz Cofer"s "Paciencia" from *The Americas Review* 16, no.2, reprinted in *The Latin Deli*, University of Georgia Press, 1993; and Pat Mora's "Senior Citizen Trio," from *Communion,* 1991.

Beacon Press for "The Old Poets of China" from *Why I Wake Early* by Mary Oliver. Copyright © 2004 by Mary Oliver.

BOA Editions, Ltd. for "miss rosie," copyright 1987 by Lucille Clifton. Reprinted from *Good Woman:* Poems and a Memoir 1969-1980.

Booklegger Press for the excerpt from *Elsa: I Come with My Songs*, 1986.

Case Western Reserve University for Geri Berg and Sally Gadow, "Towards More Human Meanings of Aging," section one, from *Aging and the Elderly,* ed. Stuart Spiker et al., Atlantic Highlands, NJ, Humanities Press, 1978.

Pearl Cleage for "Retrospect," from *Dear, Dark Faces:* Portraits of a People, ed. Helen Earle Simcox, Lotus Press, 1980.

Coffee House Press for Linda Hogan's "Drought," from *The Book of Medicines, 1993.*

COMPAS for "Red Shoes at Sixty" by Helen Earle Simcox from *Hollyhocks and Cellar Doors*: an anthology from the COMPAS literary project, St. Paul, 1988.

Ann Froines for permission to use her grandmother Anna Morgan's essay "Just Keep Breathing."

Nancy A. Henry for "Pool with Dad," first published in *Barbaric Yawp*, Sept. 2000.

Heyday Books for "Grandfather's Prayer," from *The Way We Lived:* California Indian Reminiscences, Poems, and Stories, ed. Malcolm Margolin,

1981; and for William Oandasan's essay "Grandma Jessie," from *News from Native California*, vol. 2, No.4, Sept/Oct. 1988.

Hurricane Alice for Marilyn Boe's "Birthday Check," from Vol.5, No.1, 1987.

Harcourt for Alice Walker's "The Welcome Table," from *In Love and Trouble:* Stories of Black Women, 1973.

Adair Lara for "There She Goes," originally published in the *San Francisco Chronicle*.

Nancy Manahan, literary executor of Josephine Alexander, for the essays "On Life, Death, and My Cadaver" and "A Sort of Death."

Brian Miles for permission to publish the poem "Concert" by Josephine Miles.

Midwest Villages & Voices for "The Blessings of Solomon" by Irene Paull, from *Irene:* Selected Writings of Irene Paull, ed. Gayla Ellis et al., 1996. The story was originally published in *Jewish Currents*, May 1960.

North Star Press of St. Cloud, Minnesota, publishers of the first edition of *Fierce with Reality* in 1995.

Parallax Press for "The Five Remembrances" [attributed to Buddha] from *Plum Village Chanting and Recitation Book* by Thich Nhat Hanh (2000).

Passager for "Those Wild Fauves" by Tillie Friedenberg, Winter 2006 issue.

Puckerbrush Review for Susan Pelletier's "For My Grandmother Marie-Anne Maillet," reprinted in Pelletier's *A Sense of Place*/Collected Maine Poems (Bay River Press, 2002); and for Jacqueline Moore's "Window Watching," *Puckerbrush Review* IV, No.2 (1982).

Donald Raiche, President of Apple Farm Community, for Helen Luke's "King Lear," from *Old Age*, Parabola Press, 1987.

Random House/Doubleday for three poems from *Zen Poems of China and Japan*, tr. Lucian Syryk, 1973.

Ida VSW Red for "Seasoning," from *Sinister Wisdom*, No. 53, Summer/Fall, 1994.

Jane Rule for "Free to Live," from *A Hot-Eyed Moderate.* Naiad Press, 1985.

University of Georgia Press for Margaret Walker Alexander's "Lineage," from *This is My Century*: New and Collected Poems, 1989.

Gloria Wade-Gayles for a shortened version of "Who Says an Older Woman Can't/Shouldn't Dance," from her book *Rooted Against the Wind*, Beacon Press, 1996.

Lise Weil, literary executor of Mary Meigs, for "Memory is as Uncertain as Grace."

The World Prayers Project, Santa Cruz, CA, for "Tewa Prayer."

I thank my English as a Second Language students from City College of San Francisco for their part in this book.

I also thank Isabelle Maynard, Donna Murphy, and the late Constance Hunting, editor of *Puckerbrush Review*. For making the revised edition possible, I thank Nancy Randolph of Just Write Books.

Table of Contents

Strength & Wisdom

Aging is Not for Sissies

Growth & Change

Defiance & Self-Determination

Loss

Humor

Ageism

The Fountain of Youth: Two Asian Versions

Reflections

Introduction

"If at seventy I still plant trees,
Lookers-on, do not laugh at my folly.
It is true of course that no one lives forever;
But nothing is gained by knowing so in advance."
—Yuan Mei

In the eleven years since *Fierce with Reality* was first published, aging has gained a higher profile in America but predominantly negative images of old age remain embedded in our culture. Public discussion of aging centers on Social Security and Medicare—aging as a problem or a disease—obscuring the many other facets of late life. As a result, the complexities of old age are understood mainly by those who are over sixty-five.

The main character of May Sarton's novel *As We Are Now* compares old age to another country, one not interesting until we arrive there. Perhaps many of the young and middle-aged lack the imaginative power or inclination to see themselves as old. An exception is Margaret Laurence, whose *Stone Angel* is one of the best fictional portraits of a woman at the end of her life. Before she fully conceived this novel, Laurence wrote to a friend:

> *Old age is something which interests me more and more—the myriad ways people meet it, some pretending it doesn't exist, some terrified by every physical deterioration because that final appointment is something they cannot face, some trying to balance the demands and routine of this life with an increasing need to gather together the threads of the spirit so that when the thing comes they will be ready.*

Writing in the late nineteen-century, Mary Wilkins Freeman and Sarah Orne Jewett created independent-spirited older women who foreshadow contemporary depictions by Alice Walker, Alice Munro, Tillie Olson, Doris Grumbach, and others. But even a writer as original and iconoclastic as Susan Sontag judged old age "a shipwreck."

The limits of conventional thought about aging can also be illustrated by the recently-popular phrase "anti-aging medicine," which reduces the multi-dimensional process of aging to physical signs. Here youth is assumed to be the desirable state, against which the no-longer-young must measure themselves. "Let's Pretend," the name of a 1940s Saturday morning radio program, could be the motto of those who fight a natural process with face lifts and botox.

Since the first edition of *Fierce with Reality* was published, my view of the category "old" has changed. What seemed an all-encompassing designation now appears to disguise or hide as much as it reveals. People over seventy are extremely diverse; less obvious is the arbitrariness of "the old" classification as if chronological age held primary significance. Ethnicity, gender, and class create distinctions among "the old," as does health status, so many distinctions in fact that the category "old" may not be meaningful in and of itself. At present, though "old" remains a potent signifier, its usefulness as an identity can be challenged. Why, then, separate literature about aging from literature in general? Because this stage of the lifecourse has been more stigmatized than illuminated and also because literary images of "the old," when skillfully and unsentimentally rendered, engage our emotions.

In English and American literature, however, depictions of late life have often been unrelievedly negative, for example, Matthew Arnold"s vision of old age as a time "When we are frozen up within, and quite/The phantom of ourselves." Archibald MacLeish's compared old men to dead leaves, and Louise Bogan characterized "the woman who has grown old" as a "stem long hardened/A weed that no scythe mows." Not *a* woman, an individual who may be frozen up within, but *the* woman.

The old are often portrayed stereotypically, as miserly, cranky, obsessed by sex but sexless, incompetent, drunken, bitter, childish, demented, and worthless because they may soon die. Against the materialistic measure of "productivity," those no longer working for money seem *worth less*. The dramatic shift to an aging population will not in itself be enough to create more subtle attitudes, but now that more people are surviving to old age and writing about their experiences, readers may find more truthful and complex portraits of late life.

Ageist stereotypes are especially toxic for women, already devalued to varying degrees according to their class, ethnicity, and sexual orientation. While most older women experience similar physical changes and losses and face the expectation of caregiving (challenges that may be overwhelming), each one's experience of aging is unique, and for some women, late life brings new freedoms.

Colette, for example, writes that a time comes for a woman when "the only thing that is left for her is to enrich her own self." For her one way is moving slowly: "My years and my infirmities have surely earned me the right to go slow, to stop at whim beside a narcissus, a purple orchis, or a wild strawberry." In *Sister Age*, M.F.K. Fisher acknowledges that while some aspects of aging are "scary," the process is "part of most of our lives, and it remains one we try to ignore until it seems to pounce upon us."

Now the oldest state, Maine is full of residents noting that old age has pounced upon them. They live long lives because they stay active, according to Doris Grumbach in *Coming into the End Zone*, a memoir she wrote at seventy. When a neighbor referred to a friend dead at eighty-one as having died prematurely, Grumbach comments, "Not to reach ninety up here is regarded as a disappointing act of carelessness or accident."

By contrast, many Black women writers have not lived to be sixty, a great loss for American literature. How would women such as Audre Lorde, June Jordan, Barbara Christian, Barbara Jordan, Pat Parker, Toni Cade Bambera and Olivia Butler have described their aging process? In the introduction to her collection *Grand Mothers*, Nikki Giovanni, writes that grandmothers are "a lot like spinach or asparagus or brussels sprouts: something good for us that we appreciate much more in reflection than in actuality… [but] they are always on our side."

Anthologies of literature about aging offer images of late life that transcend the disease-problem-shipwreck model that shrinks old age to an undesirable or dreaded condition. Valuable in themselves as works that give pleasure, they also strongly counteract prevailing cultural attitudes. Losses and challenges faced by many of the old—death of a spouse or partner, for example—are not glossed over by writers in these anthologies, and indignities suffered by the old are also vividly portrayed. While medical science and the social sciences deal with measurable aspects of aging—sometimes misleadingly—literature opens up its mysteries.

Fierce with Reality is a miscellany, created in the spirit of that nineteen-century form, literally "a mixture of various things." Implicit in the choice of work is the notion that the old are more interesting and less categorizable than readers of social science or mainstream books and articles may have noticed. The mixture here is idiosyncratic, to be sure, and many aspects of aging are not treated. The anthology evolved over several years, with works written especially for this anthology taking their place with previously-published stories, articles, and poems. The new edition includes several poems and stories by Maine writers.

Fierce with Reality features writers from many cultural traditions and mixes folk tales, personal narratives, and fiction with analytical essays. The anthology is divided into these sections: A Kaleiscope of Images, Homage to Grandmothers, Strength and Wisdom, "Aging is not for Sissies" (the title of a 1975 book by Terry Schuckman), Growth and Change, Defiance and Self-Determination, Humor, Ageism, Loss, The Fountain of Youth: Two Asian Versions, and Reflections.

Most contributors to this book regard old age as a fruitful time of life, to be celebrated rather than lamented. They would agree with Andre Gide who wrote that "A fine old age can never be taken for granted. It represents perpetual victories and perpetual recoveries from defeat." Such sharp contrasts do not do justice to our aging, idiosyncratic selves, however, or to the myriad strands of old age, knit, unraveled, and knit again. "This is the best time of my life," Willie Nelson told interviewer Connie Goldman, "just that I made it this far, I'm still here, and I'm still healthy. The older I get, the better I feel about things."

I hope that the liveliness, variety, and humor of this anthology will appeal to readers and that even its bleak passages will suggest to those under seventy that the country of the old is not a forbidding or alien territory. As for the old themselves, who already know that, the anthology may mirror some of their own experiences or suggest new ways of thinking about aging.

They have made it this far; they are still here.

Margaret Cruikshank

References

Yuan Mei, excerpt from "Seven Poems on Aging" translated by Arthur Waley. In *Middle Age, Old Age,* ed. Ruth Granetz Lyell. Harcourt, Brace, Jovanovich, 1980.

Other references in the Introduction in the order cited are:

May Sarton, *As We Are Now.* Norton, 1973, p. 17.

Donez Xiques, *Margaret Laurence. The Making of a Writer.* Dundurn Press, 2005, p. 234.

Susan Sontag, "The Double Standard of Aging," in *The Other Within: Feminist Explorations of Women and Aging,* ed. Marilyn Pearsall. Westview, 1997.

Matthew Arnold, "Growing Old," in *Middle Age, Old Age: Short Stories, Poems, Plays, and Essays on Aging,* ed. Ruth Granetz Lyell. Harcourt, Brace, Jovanovich, 1980.

Archibald MacLeish, "The Old Men in Leaf Smoke," in *Collected Poems.* Houghton Mifflin, 1985.

Louise Bogan, "The Crows," in *No More Masks. An anthology of poetry by women,* eds. Florence Howe and Ellen Bass. Anchor Doubleday, 1973.

Colette, *Break of Day,* tr. Enid McLeod and *The Blue Lantern,* tr. Roger Senhouse. Farrar, Straus, Giroux, 1963. The first quotation is from *Break of Day,* p. 34; the second from *The Blue Lantern,* p. 27.

M.F.K. Fisher, *Sister Age,* Vintage, 1984, p. 245.

Nikki Giovanni, Introduction to *Grand Mothers. Poems, Reminiscences, and Short Stories about the Keepers of Our Traditions.* Henry Holt, 1994, p. xvii.

Doris Grumbach, *Coming into the End Zone.* Norton, 1991, p. 234.

Willie Nelson, In *The Ageless Spirit: Reflections on living life to the fullest in midlife and the years beyond,* ed. Connie Goldman. Fairview Press, 2004, p. 12.

A Kaleidoscope of Images

Paciencia

The oldest woman in the village, Paciencia,
predicts the weather from the flight of birds:
Today, it will rain toads, she says,
squinting her face into a mystery of wrinkles
as she reads the sky—*tomorrow,
it will be snakes.*
      Paciencia moves
with the grace of a ghost, walking unnoticed
down the roads lined with pleading eyes
and grasping hands, clothed in the invisibility
of her great age.
      Paciencia sucks the meat of figs
with toothless gums; sleeps little—shuffling
through empty rooms at night, making order,
breathing in the dust
careless youth stirs up in passing.
She hums as she weaves an endless pattern
of intersecting lines; she cocks her head sometimes,
as if listening for her name in the wind—
the dance of her bones evident through paper-thin skin
as she works—like a bird trapped in a sack.
      And Paciencia does
what Paciencia pleases, having outlived rules.
She washes the limbs of the dead tenderly as babies
being readied for a nap; comforts the widows.
And while the world around her flames and freezes,
she tends the graves of the ones she remembers,
bending closer to the earth, like an old tree,
giving shelter, giving shade.

Judith Ortiz Cofer

Judith Ortiz Cofer, poet, essayist, and novelist, has won fellowships from NEA and the Bread Loaf Writers' Conference. The title essay from her *Silent Dancing* was selected for *The Best American Essays 1991*. A native of Puerto Rico, Professor Cofer teaches English and creative writing at the University of Georgia.

Concert

I was sitting behind a somewhat neat old person
In creamlined beige matching coat and hat
Neat but that the hat crown
Tilted at a curious angle left to right.
As I deliberated, she turned her head impatiently
As at a draft of air,
And pulled the hat from off a mane of hair,
Of wild white hair.

Josephine Miles

Josephine Miles (1911-1985), poet and professor of English at the University of California, Berkeley, from 1940 to 1978, won many poetry awards. Her *Collected Poems* appeared in 1983. Her literary criticism includes *Poetry and Change: Donne, Milton, Wordsworth, and the Equilibrium of the Present* (1974). Miles was known as a gifted teacher who exerted extraordinary influence on her students. She left her house to the University of California as a poetry center.

Poems by Po Chui
translated by Arthur Waley

Old Age
(Addressed to Liu Yu-hsi, who was
born in the same year.)
(A.D. 835)

We are growing old together, you and I;
Let us ask ourselves, what is age like?
The dull eye is closed ere night comes;
The idle head, still uncombed at noon.
Propped on a staff, sometimes a walk abroad;
Or all day sitting with closed doors.

One dares not look in the mirror's polished face;
One cannot read small-letter books.
Deeper and deeper, one's love of old friends;
Fewer and fewer, one's dealings with young men.
One thing only, the pleasure of idle talk,
Is as great as ever, when you and I meet.

To Liu Yu-Hsi
(A.D. 835)

In length of days and soundness of limbs you and I are one;
Our eyes are not wholly blind, nor our ears quite deaf.
Deep drinking we lie together, fellows of a spring day;
Or gay-hearted boldly break into gatherings of young men.
When, seeking flowers, we borrowed his horse, the Governor was vexed;
When, to play on the water, we sole his boat, the Duke of Chin was sore.
I hear it said that in Lo-pang people are all shocked,
And call us by the name of "Liu and Po, those two mad old men."

Po Chui (772-846 A.D.), one of China's greatest poets, was a high-ranking official under Emperor Hsieu Tsung. After banishment and disillusionment with public life, he built a retreat for himself and several companions. Poetry and philosophy were his interests. Later he became governor of Soochow. His poems were engraved upon stone tablets.

Though You Are Yoong

Though you are yoong and I am olde,
Though your vaines hot and my bloud colde,
Though youth is moist and age is drie,
Yet embers live when flames doe die.

The tender graft is easely broke,
But who shall shake the sturdie Oke?
You are more fresh and faire then I,
Yet stubs doe live, when flowers doe die.

Thou that thy youth doest vainely boast,
Know buds are soonest nipt with frost;
Thinke that thy fortune still doth crie,
Thou foole, tomorrow thou must die.

Thomas Campion

Thomas Campion (1567-1620), English Renaissance poet, studied law before taking a medical degree. His poetry is highly musical, and his airs are regarded as among the best in English. One collaboration with a lutenist is titled *A Book of Ayres* (1601).

Pawnee Buffalo Dance Song

Listen
the song of the aged father

The song
of the aged beloved

Our father
the buffalo heavy with age

Heavy with age
endlessly walking

Too heavy
to rise again if he should fall

Walking forever
walking forever

Humped high with age
head bent with age

Heavy with age
heavy with age

Aged buffalo
my aged father

—adapted from a translation by Densmore in *Pawnee Music BAE Bulletin* 93, Washington
D.C., 1929.

Our old women gods, we ask you

Our old women gods, we ask you!
Our old women gods, we ask you!
Then give us long life together,
May we live until our frosted hair is white;
May we live till then.
This life that now we know!

American Indian—Tewa

The **Tewa** are a group of Pueblo Indians who live near the Rio Grande north of Santa Fe. Arizona Tewa live on the Hopi reservation.

Grandfather's Prayer
Wintu

For some people, it is true, old age brought pain, disappointment, even bitterness. For others, however, it brought a deep familiarity with the world, self-acceptance, even wisdom. "Long ago, when I was small," recalled a Wintu woman, "I used to listen to my grandfather when he prayed." The grandfather woke early in the morning, washed his face, and prayed. He prayed to Olelbes, He-Who-Is-Above, the Wintu world creator. He also prayed directly and intimately to the things around him—to the rocks, trees, salmon, acorns, sugar-pine, water, and wood. At the end of his life, he talked to the world—sharing his sadness and regret—as one might talk to an old and very trusted friend.*

Oh, Olelbes, look down on me.
I wash my face in water, for you,
Seeking to remain in health.
I am advancing in old age; I am not capable of anything anymore.
You whose nature it is to be eaten [i.e., deer],
You dwell high in the west, on the mountains, high in the east,
          high in the north, high in the south;
You, salmon, you go about in the water.
Yet I cannot kill you and bring you home.
Neither can I go east down the slope to fetch you, salmon.
When a man is so advanced in age, he is not in full vigor.
If you are rock, look at me; I am advancing in old age.
If you are tree, look at me; I am advancing in old age.
If you are water, look at me; I am advancing in old age.
Acorns, I can never climb up to you again.
You, water, I can never dip you up and fetch you home again.
My legs are advancing in weakness.
Sugar-pine, you sit there; I can never climb you.
In my northward arm, in my southward arm, I am advancing in weakness.
You who are wood, you wood, I cannot carry you home on my shoulder.
For I am falling back into my cradle.
This is what my ancestors told me yesterday, they have gone, long ago.
May my children fare likewise!

The reference to "northward arm" and "southward arm" was typically Wintu, and its usage, suggests a cultural wisdom so deep and unconscious that it was embedded in the very structure of language. In English we refer to the right arm and the left arm, and we might describe a certain mountain as being to our right or left, in front or back of us depending upon which way we are facing at the moment. We use the body—the self— as the point of reference against which we describe the world. The Wintu would never do this, and, indeed, the Wintu language would not permit it. If a certain mountain was to the north, say, the arm nearest that mountain would be called the northward arm. If the Wintu turned around, the arm that had previously been referred to as the northward arm would now be called the southward arm. In other words, the features of the world remained the constant reference; the sense of self was what changed—a self that continually accommodated and adjusted to a world in which the individual was not the center of all creation.*

*Notes preceding and following the poem are by **Malcolm Margolin**. The Wintu tribe lived in northern California.

This work is from **Dorothy D. Lee,** "Some Indian Texts Dealing with the Supernatural," *Review of Religion* 5 (1941): 407. The prayer was recalled by a granddaughter, **Sadie Marsh.**

Those Wild Fauves

He dozes in his easy chair,
On his lap *Art and Society* opened
To the section on Fauve painters.
Ten minutes into his book,
He has slipped into his afternoon nap.
I am careful not to disturb him.

Waking, he sits upright,
Closes the book, says something like,
"Boy, those Fauves were some wild bunch,"
As though he had been reading.
"Did you have a good nap?" I ask.
"What nap? he insists. "I don't take naps."

Someday I should like to grow into a greater kindness.
When he says, "Boy, those Fauves were some wild bunch,"
I will reply, "They certainly were."
He will tell me what a great nap he had.

Tillie Friedenberg

Tillie Friedenberg, a retired speech and language pathologist, started writing when she was over seventy. She now lives in Charlestown Retirement Community and works with the Poems for Peace project with children in Baltimore. Excited to be writing again, she believes she could not have written "Those Wild Fauves" when she was twenty.

Old Woman in Triumph

She climbs mountains with the hardiness of granite,
        gentleness of ferns.
Waterfall spray beads her lashes with color.
Meditations reflect in mirror lake.

Sequoias lead her vision to where the sky begins—
        clouds, flocks of white doves.
In the valley, when raindrops splash poppies,
        she studies magnified pores in orange reverie.

Her landscapes are varied, challenging:
        She explores deserts: sage, mud cracks,
                ocotillo, horned toad,
                        blueness of the Panamints.
        Notes made on tumbleweed blow back
                across the dunes, leaning into moonlight.

        At ocean beach, she gathers shells;
        washing off the sand and dust, she fingers
        rainbows … sea breeze, wind from wings of
                a thousand gulls.

When her landscapes are veiled and murky,
she yields herself calmly to shadows,
remembering to remember that shadows are cast by
the sun.

Claire J. Baker

Claire J. Baker was a 2004 grand prize winner at the Dancing Poetry Festival, sponsored by Artists Embassy International, at San Francisco's Palace of the Legion of Honor. Her prize poem, "Double Helix," was choreographed and performed at this event. Baker is active in the northern California poetry scene.

The Welcome Table

for sister Clara Ward

Alice Walker

The old woman stood with eyes uplifted in her Sunday-go-to-meeting clothes: high shoes polished about the tops and toes, a long rusty dress adorned with an old corsage, long withered, and the remnants of an elegant silk scarf as headrag stained with grease from the many oily pigtails underneath. Perhaps she had known suffering. There was a dazed and sleepy look in her aged blue-brown eyes. But for those who searched hastily for "reasons" in that old tight face, shut now like an ancient door, there was nothing to be read. And so they gazed nakedly upon their own fear transferred; a fear of the black and the old, a terror of the unknown as well as of the deeply known. Some of those who saw her there on the church steps spoke words about her that were hardly fit to be heard, others held their pious peace; and some felt vague stirrings of pity, small and persistent and hazy, as if she were an old collie turned out to die.

She was angular and lean and the color of poor gray Georgia earth, beaten by king cotton and the extreme weather. Her elbows were wrinkled and thick, the skin ashen but durable, like the bark of old pines. On her face centuries were folded into the circles around one eye, while around the other, etched and mapped as if for print, ages more threatened again to live. Some of them there at the church saw the age, the dotage, the missing buttons down the front of her mildewed black dress. Others saw cooks, chauffeurs, maids, mistresses, children denied or smothered in the deferential way she held her cheek to the side, toward the ground. Many of them saw jungle orgies in an evil place, while others were reminded of riotous anarchists looting and raping in the streets. Those who knew the hesitant creeping up on them of the law, saw the beginning of the end of the sanctuary of Christian worship, saw the desecration of Holy Church, and saw an invasion of privacy, which they struggled to believe they still kept.

Still she had come down the road toward the big white church alone. Just herself, an old forgetful woman, nearly blind with age. Just her and her eyes raised dully to the glittering cross that crowned the sheer silver steeple. She had walked along the road in a stagger from her house a half mile away. Perspiration, cold and clammy, stood on her brow and along the creases by her thin wasted nose. She stopped to calm herself on the wide front steps, not looking about her as they might have expected her to do, but simply standing quite still, except for a slight quivering of her throat and tremors that shook her cotton-stockinged legs.

The reverend of the church stopped her pleasantly as she stepped into the vestibule. Did he say, as they thought he did, kindly, "Auntie, you know this is not your church?" As if one could choose the wrong one. But no one remembers, for they never spoke of it afterward, and she brushed past him anyway, as if she had been brushing past him all her life, except this time she was in a hurry. Inside the church, she sat on the very first bench from the back, gazing with concentration at the stained-glass window over her head. It was cold, even inside the church, and she was shivering. Everybody could see. They stared at her as they came in and sat down near the front. It was cold, very cold to them, too; outside the church it was below freezing and now much above inside. But the sight of her, sitting there somehow passionately ignoring them, brought them up short, burning.

The young usher, never having turned anyone out of his church before, but not even considering this job as *that* (after all, she had no right to be there, certainly), went up to her and whispered that she should leave. Did he call her "Grandma," as later he seemed to recall he had? But for those who actually heard such traditional pleasantries and to whom they actually mean something, "Grandma" was not one, for she did not pay him any attention, just muttered, "Go 'way," in weak sharp *bothered* voice, waving his frozen blond hair and eyes from near her face.

It was the ladies who finally did what to them had to be done. Daring their burly indecisive husbands to throw the old colored woman out, they made their point. God, mother, country, earth, church. It involved all that, and well they knew it. Leather bagged and shoed, with good calfskin gloves to keep out the cold, they looked with contempt at the bloodless gray arthritic hands of the old woman, clenched loosely, restlessly in her lap. Could their husbands expect them to sit up in church with *that*? No, no, the husbands were quick to answer and even quicker to do their duty.

Under the old woman's arms, they placed their hard fists (which afterward smelled of decay and musk–the fermenting scent of onion skins and rotting greens). Under the old woman's arms they raised their fists, flexed their muscular shoulders, and out she flew through the doors, back under the cold blue sky. This done, the wives folded their healthy arms across their trim middles and felt at once justified and scornful. But none of them said so, for none of them ever spoke of the incident again. Inside the church it was warmer. They sang, they prayed. The protection and promise of God's impartial love grew more not less desirable as the sermon gathered fury and lashed itself out above their penitent heads.

The old woman stood at the top of the steps looking about in bewilderment. She had been singing in her head. They had interrupted her. Promptly she began to sing again, though his time a sad song. Suddenly, however, she looked down the long gray highway and saw something interesting and delightful coming. She started to grin, toothlessly, with short giggles of joy, jumping about and slapping her hands on her knees. And soon it became apparent why she was so happy. For coming down the highway at a firm though leisurely pace was Jesus. He was wearing an immaculate white, long dress trimmed in gold around the neck and hem, and a red, a bright red, cape. Over his left arm he carried a brilliant blue blanket. He was wearing sandals and a beard, and he had long brown hair parted on the right side. His eyes, brown, had wrinkles around them as if he smiled or looked at the sun a lot. She would have known him, recognized him, anywhere. There was a sad but joyful look to his face, like a candle was glowing behind it, and he walked with sure even steps in her direction, as if he were walking on the sea. Except that he was not carrying in his arms a baby sheep, he looked exactly like the picture of him that she had hanging over her bed at home. She had taken it out of a white lady's Bible while she was working for her. She had looked at that picture for more years than she could remember, but never once had she really expected to see him. She squinted her eyes to be sure he wasn't carrying a little sheep in one arm, but he was not. Ecstatically she began to wave her arms for fear he would miss seeing her, for he walked looking straight ahead on the shoulder of the highway, and from time to time looking upward at the sky.

All he said when he got up close to her was "Follow me," and she bounded down to his side with all the bob and speed of one so old. For every one of his long determined steps, she made two quick ones. They walked along in deep silence for a long time. Finally she started telling him about how many years she had cooked for them, cleaned for them, nursed them. He looked at her kindly but in silence. She told him indignantly about how they had grabbed her when she was singing in her head and not looking, and how they had tossed her out of his church. A old heifer like me, she said, straightening up next to Jesus, breathing hard. But he smiled down at her, and she felt better instantly, and time just seemed to fly by. When they passed her house, forlorn and sagging, weatherbeaten and patched, by the side of the road, she did not even notice it, she was so happy to be out walking along the highway with Jesus.

She broke the silence once more to tell Jesus how glad she was that he had come, how she had often looked at his picture hanging on her wall (she hoped he didn't know she had stolen it) over her bed, and how she had never expected to see him down here in person. Jesus gave her one of his beautiful smiles, and they walked on. She did not know where they were going; someplace wonderful, she suspected. The ground was like clouds under their feet, and she felt she could walk forever without becoming the least bit tired. She even began to sing out loud some of the old spirituals she loved, but she didn't want to annoy Jesus, who looked so thoughtful, so she quieted down. They walked on, looking straight over the treetops into the sky, and the smiles that played over her dry wind-cracked face were like first clean ripples across a stagnant pond. On they walked without stopping.

⌣

The people in church never knew what happened to the old woman; they never mentioned her to one another or to anybody else. Most of them heard sometime later that an old colored woman fell dead along the highway. Silly as it seemed, it appeared she had walked herself to death. Many of the black families along the road said they had seen the old lady high-stepping down the highway; sometimes jabbering in a low insistent voice, sometimes singing, sometimes merely gesturing excitedly with her hands. Other times silent and smiling, looking at the sky. She had been alone, they said, Some of them wondered aloud where the old woman had been going so stoutly that it had worn her heart out. They guessed maybe she had relatives across the river, some miles away, but none of them really knew.

Alice Walker, poet, novelist, and essayist, is one of the best known writers in America today. In 1983, her novel *The Color Purple* won both the Pulitzer Prize and the American Book Award. *In Search of Our Mothers' Gardens* recovers the work of African artists. Other books include *Living by the Word: Selected Writings 1973-1987* and *Warrior Marks: Female Genital Mutilation and the Blinding of Women* (1993), with Patibha Parmar. Walker lives in northern California. The collection from which "The Welcome Table" is taken, *In Love and Trouble*, contains another excellent portrait of aging, "To Hell with Dying."

Homage to Grandmothers

Matmiya
(for my Grandmother)

I see you sitting
Implanted by roots
Coiled deep from your thighs.
Roots, flesh, red, centuries pale.
Hairsprings wound tight
Through fertile earthscapes
Where each layer feeds the next
Into depths immutable.

Though you must rise, must
Move large and slow
When it is time, O my
Gnarled mother-vine, ancient
As vanished ages,
Your spirit remains
Nourished,
Nourishing me.

I see your figure wrapped in skins
Curved into a mound of earth
Holding your rich dark roots.
Matmiya,
I see you sitting.

Mary TallMountain

Mary TallMountain (1918-1994), a Native American of Koyukon-Athabaskan descent, was born in 1918. She was a long-time resident of San Francisco, but the Yukon river was her "spirit's home." For more than twenty years, she was active in the Native American literature renaissance. Bill Moyers featured her on his PBS poetry series *The Power of the Word*. She wrote two books: *The Light on the Tent Wall* (UCLA Press, 1990) and *A Quick Brush of Wings* (Freedom Voices, 1991).

Grandma Jessie
William Oandasan

In "Grandmothers Land," the dedication poem of my *Round Valley Songs,* I have written of my great-grandmother Jessie. She was the first grandmother in my family to reside on the allotment land described in the poem, and she began living there but five generations ago. An image of her and me is still perfect in my memory from a time in my youth more than thirty years ago. I was wearing my usual striped t-shirt, blue levis, and black, high-top, Converse tennis shoes, with my hair cut in a bushy flat-top and my two front teeth prominently showing. Her rotund body filled her customary black dress around which she always wore an apron when at home. Her black nylon stockings rose from her black Buster Brown shoes with medium heels to where they were held by plain garters just below the knees. Her face was round with high cheek bones, like a classic California face, and her skin was smooth and very dark, like the endless depths of her eyes. Her black hair (although graying) was always rolled into a bun at the back of her head, and I never saw her long hair, which hung to mid-back in length, until she let it down for brushing each evening before bedtime or before starting each day.

One summer we had lived alone in Round Valley. I was supposed to help her by chopping wood for the kitchen stove, pumping and carrying water, and walking with her to Covelo for kerosene for the lamps at night. I remember rising from sleep every morning to hear singing birds with feathers of black, red, yellow, brown, and beige. They perched in various patterns on the electric wires strung between the telephone poles running along the dirt lane across from the yard on the west side of our unpainted redwood home. Those birds in the morning and Grandma Jessie at night have been some of my first experiences connecting music, songs, and stories. Over the years, those intimate associations have evolved, I tend to believe, into *Round Valley Songs* and "Grandmothers Land."

During those summer nights, like many other times for those few years that I knew her, Grandma Jessie would sing songs and tell stories to me. Nowadays I wish that I knew those stories and tales, but they are only memories of memories now, like the wild herbs and teas that she had taught me to gather in the woods bordering her ten acres on the east side where a creek ran south from north through a marsh. In the quiet of her redwood house, with shadows from the kerosene lamp dancing on the walls and ceiling of the bedroom, she would tell me stories in English. The songs, however, must have been in Yuki, our mother language, because I did not understand a word of them, just the soft sounds of her voice and the rhythms that seemed to hum me to sleep. Those cadences, narratives, and sounds do not appear in my Round Valley poems, but the poetry embodies the spirit of those nights and mornings of that summer long ago. They are also a link with the last days of the "old time," of which Grandma Jessie, in her youth, was one of the last witnesses, and with these days in which I am living.

Grandma Jessie was one of the latest carriers of the knowledge of the old Yukian ways. She was born in the last decade of the nineteenth century when our tribal traditions were quickly coming to an end. She was one of our family who was able to conduct the last, if not one of the most recent, puberty rites of the tribe, which was for my mother. She, George Moore, Little Toby (one of the last Yukian shamans), and his wife Lizzy formed the extended family for my mother when she was left behind by her mother who went to make another family. They were some of the informants for George Foster's book summarizing Yukian culture and Cora DuBois' book on the 1870 and 1890 ghost dances in northern California, both volumes having been published by the University of California at Berkeley. Foster and DuBois used to consult with the family at Grandma Jessie's home, and DuBois went so far as to state in her book that George and Toby were her most reliable sources of information in Round Valley. I recall that day in 1956 as vividly as I recollect the rural summer when she and I bonded forever with each other, where I, and over a hundred people, watched her being lowered into the land of the Yuki since time immemorial.

In addition to the description in my selective service file of how I had learned a form of compassion from her example, Grandma Jessie's singing and storytelling have provided significant gifts toward my life as a poet. I can now see how the songs and tales had helped to create love and respect within me for words, and, since then, for imaginative and thoughtful writing. During those nights without radio and television, her melodies and narratives were boundless containers of sound, sense, and invention, like epic poems or folk songs crafted by poets and singers and carried on tongues from generation to generation.

I remember how the sounds once made me realize that Grandma Jessie was at one in thought and feeling with the sources from which she was drawing a song, though the song was only her melody to me. Her voice was clear and confidently unselfconscious but for the act of singing. She did not expel but released the sounds into the night like so many musical notes looking for morning's light. She sang as if she herself might have been, to me, a songbird. I remember how she would keep my attention when telling a story by using an unusual twist of plot, an unexpected word, a vivid image, a cluster of words resonating through their related meanings, the parallel repetition of phrases, or, maybe, another clever use of language. I remember during the few times when I did not go immediately to sleep that Grandma Jessie, after she had sung the lyrics and completed the tales, would recite a short prayer in Yuki, then briefly recite a Christian prayer for me in English before she doused the kerosene lamp and went to sleep. I remember, too, the secure feeling that she expressed in her voice–a peacefulness of mind, emotion, and active Being that rarely comes nowadays with old age.

Grandma Jessie probably had never thought of herself as an artist or a teacher, but she knew what she knew and what she knew was what she had learned, and much of what she had learned was passed to her through the oral traditions of our people. Still, she knew arithmetic, spoke fluent Yuki and English and some Spanish, plus wrote and read in English. She had some knowledge, too, of real estate practices, since she had acquired hundreds of acres, sold some of them to the lumber industry, even dictated in her will how they would be distributed. She also had had the mind and spirit to adapt to Christianity without self-conflict, while heartfully embracing her Yukian ancestry, and to have the attendance of prominent businessmen and pastors in the community as well as of scholars from the University of California at her rustic redwood house where she made a home for her family.

There are other memories of Grandma Jessie that I will probably take with me into my next existence. Those memories are as clear to me as family photographs. I can see her now beside the house where she spent her very last days west of Sebastopol along the highway leading to the sea, leaching acorn meal in preparation for her favorite dish of hot cereal. She is standing in a dark dress with a light blue apron hemmed with white linen, over a cloth stretched about a foot above the ground between four stakes, pouring water into acorn meal and stirring it with a wooden spoon while water leached the tannin when it dripped from the bottom of the cloth.

Or, the time that she made one of her concessions to modern convenience when my father taught her how to make ground beef with the meat grinder that he had bought for her because she would not consent to having dentures. Although her lips only showed a bare twist of a smile, I can still see the tightening wrinkles at the corners of her eyes that showed the appreciation for the concern of my father for her. She had held her arms proudly folded just below her bosom as she stood facing him, and the men and women had stood still around them, watching and listening. My father was speaking to her with his low-pitched voice punctuated with heavy Ilocano accents.

It is these images of respect, independence, and stern compassion that have caused me, I believe, to be stubbornly unrelenting in my writing, in the public arena, and on the job. But I will be as proud of my actions as I am of these fond memories of Grandma Jessie.

Grandmothers Land

around the house stood an
orchard of plum, apple and pear
a black walnut tree, one white pine,
groves of white oak and willow clumps
the home of Jessie was largely redwood

blood, flesh and bone sprouted
inside her womb of redwood
for five generations
the trees now stand unpruned and wild

after relocating so many years before
the War
the seeds of Jessie have returned

afternoon sunlight on the field
breezes moving grass and leaves
memories with family names wait
within the earth, the mountains,
the valley, the field, the trees

William Oandasan (1947-1992) was a member of the Yuki tribe at the Round Valley reservation in Northern California. His book *Round Valley Songs*, published by West End Press in Minneapolis, won an American Book Award from the Before Columbus Foundation in 1985. His poetry is included in *Harper's Anthology of 20th Century native American Poetry*. One of his interests was the synthesis of native oral traditions with contemporary literature.

Lineage

My grandmothers were strong.
They followed plows and bent to toil.
They moved through fields sowing seed.
They touched earth and grain grew.
They were full of sturdiness and singing.
My grandmothers were strong.

My grandmothers are full of memories
Smelling of soap and onions and wet clay
With veins rolling roughly over quick hands
They have many clean words to say.
My grandmothers were strong.
Why am I not as they?

Margaret Walker

Margaret Walker (1915-1998), professor of English at Jackson State University in Mississippi from 1949 until 1979, won the Yale Younger Poets award in 1942. She established the Institute for the Study of Black Life and Culture in 1968. Her biography of Richard Wright was published in 1988, followed two years later by *How I Wrote Jubilee and Other Essays on Life and Literature*. Her last book, *Being Female, Black, and Free*, was published in 1997.

For My Grandmother, Marie-Anne Maillet

Mémère
If you were alive
This morning
I would bring you
(In your cool kitchen)
A bowl
Of red raspberries

You would put down
Your book and say
"Qu'elles sont belles!"
Hold the brimming bowl
In your two hands
Like a face you loved,
Lift it to your nose,
Your mouth

If you were alive
This morning
I might tell you
How your joy
Awaiting me
Cleared each brambly cane
In my way

Susann Pelletier

Susan Pelletier, a Lewiston native, gives voice to her deep connections to Franco-America, as well as to her vision of social justice and dignity at home and beyond our borders. Her articles and poems have been published here and abroad in anthologies, literary journals, chapbooks, and political and environmental magazines. She currently works as an instructor at the Writing Workshop at Bates College.

Free to Live

Jane Rule

My little grandmother who had everything wrong with her, arthritis, phlebitis, anemia, to say nothing about her nerves, said to me, "The one thing I don't want to do is lose my mind. As long as I have my mind …" She used it mostly for playing cards, the horses, memorizing the words to her favorite songs, and bugging my mother. Nevertheless, she thought her mind was important to her. And she did, in the last year of her life, lose it. At first she only wrote cheques on banks where she didn't have accounts and phoned us in cities where we didn't live, but gradually hallucinations took over her days and nights, mostly in bizarre sexual forms. Then she was convinced she was in a motel or rest home or hospital, and she begged to be taken home, not to the house where she then, in fact, lived but to her childhood home, to her parents, sisters, and brother. Reclusive as a result of illness and fear, she hadn't gone out socially for years. People kept sending her invitations because she refused them with flowers. Now, after twenty years, she began to accept those invitations, and members of the family had to take her to garden and cocktail parties of the retired military, the garden club. She swung in on the arm of a grandchild, wielding her cane, found a place to sit and raffled off the cherry in her Old Fashioned to other bemused and ailing old people.

Once, on the way home from one of those parties, she said to me, "Do you remember how I used to say to you I was afraid of losing my mind?"

"Yes," I answered cautiously.

"Well, it's not so bad," she replied. "I think: Is that the world I was afraid of for all those years? Is that all it is?"

Divorced when it was not the thing to be divorced, married a second time to an alcoholic she wouldn't divorce because a second time around would prove she was at fault, my little grandmother had to lose her mind to lose her shame, to be free of all that social garbage. Her last night of consciousness, she sang every song she'd ever known, and my mother sang with her, everything from "Dixie Dan, ambling, rambling, gambling minstrel man" to "You'll Never Walk Alone" and "To Kiss in the Sunlight," two favorites of mine as well, since I was also afraid of my loneliness and the secrecy imposed upon my heart.

As I watch so many of my friends reclusive in fear, defending their silence and lies, I understand that I am, in an odd way, my little grandmother gone crazy, not to be free to die but to be free to live. I want to say, in my turn, "It's not so bad. The terrifying, judgmental world out there isn't all it's cracked up to be. It can be maneuvered with a kid and a cane." Because of my little grandmother, I didn't wait to be lame as I sometimes am now to walk in the world. Her beloved bad example sent me crazy brave when I still walked without help. Like her, I was afraid, and I fell, broke courage, bones, but, because of her, I knew it was my fear that crippled, nothing else.

Nearly everything that I was once deathly afraid of has happened to me. I lost my beloved woman to her moral scruples. No one would publish my work for ten years, and I was nearly as frightened of my eventual success as I was of my failure. When my third novel was finally accepted by a publisher, I had no idea how much of my world I was risking. I kept my teaching job. Of my family, only my younger sister wanted to disown me for a while. The several friends I lost were gay and afraid to be seen any longer in my company.

I had published several novels and *Lesbian Images* before national magazines began doing profiles on me, ostensibly because I am a writer but really because I am a lesbian. Every time one of these comes out, I get letters, hate mail, cries for help, love letters, religious tracts. Many more people read journalistic junk than they do books. The greatest horror for most closeted people is to be publicly exposed, never again to be known as a writer or teacher or parent but always to be identified as a lesbian and, therefore, discredited.

The fear is far worse than the fact. Even the polls say that over fifty percent of Canadians think gay people should have civil rights, and most people don't care much one way or the other. The parents it would kill live on, and siblings gradually gain new tolerance and understanding. Each year the sexual orientation clause is added to another union contract. If all else fails, there are always jobs at the post office.

The benefits are enormous. Once the very worst has happened, there's nothing left to be afraid of that isn't the common lot. The energy that fed anxiety can be turned instead to work, to love, to telling the truth, whose ring is very sweet after years of silence and lying. If there is an anticlimax in finding that one is not, after all, a martyr but, in the words of one of our since dead national magazines, "simply a human being." It is a letdown we can live with happily. "Is that all it is?" my little grandmother asked. That's all.

Jane Rule is a distinguished Canadian novelist, essayist, short story writer and gay rights activist. Her 1987 novel *Memory Board* treats dementia with insight and grace. *Fiction and Other Truths*, a film about Jane Rule, was released in 1995. She lives on Galiano Island, B.C.

Strength & Wisdom

Old Age in Vietnamese Culture: Two Views
Dahn Ho and Tan Luong

Dahn Ho

The difference between Western culture and Vietnamese culture regarding old age is the way we think about it. Here, old age is the ending stage of life, while in Vietnamese culture, old age is not thought of as the beginning of the end but rather as a separate stage of life. During this time, life is not measured by physical strength or physical activity but in terms of the wisdom one is rewarded in growing old. A very popular saying from Vietnamese literature is "hoa tan, qua dom," which can be translated into English as "when a flower withers, a bud is forming."

Though the old are generally not regarded as people of strength in Vietnamese culture, they are considered not only as the sources of wisdom accumulated from experiences but also as the possessors of toughness. That is why family life in Vietnam revolves around the old. They are the ultimate deciders in the family. Often they are glorified in sayings such as "trau gia, trau cui," which means "old water buffaloes are the strongest," or "tre gia, tre cung," which means "the older the bamboo, the stronger the bamboo," or "gia khon voi tuoi," which means "wisdom is growing with age." Old bamboo may not have much juice inside, but it is tough and hard with its ripened fibers.

Aging to Westerners is a youth robber (I will think so if I pass the twenty-five year mark) as we often say I am so and so years old, while to a Vietnamese, aging is a reward. This is reflected in our language: we Vietnamese often say I am given so and so number of springs when we tell our age. I suspect this usage reflects the high mortality rate in Vietnam. To grow old is a good thing; one has beaten death, at least for now, the death many others have succumbed to. To live to old age is to be blessed by high Heaven. That is why old people often say to the young, "kinh lao, dac tho," which means "pay respect to the old, and you will be rewarded with longevity." No wonder in Vietnam the custom of asking people their age is very popular; it is a way of inquiring into the other person's blessing and a way to praise their luck, though rather subtly. So don't be shocked when you visit Vietnam and nine out of ten Vietnamese you meet ask you how old you are.

Our attitude toward aging, like the rest of our culture, is heavily influenced by Buddhism. Youth and old age are not a big matter for the Vietnamese as they often are for Westerners. Many Vietnamese feel that death is a way to return to our roots, to where we come from, for we often say, "chet la tro ve voi cat bui," which means "dying is to go back to ash and dust." Getting old is to come closer to death, closer to the ultimate root. Since many Vietnamese believe in reincarnation, aging for them is only a part of the cycle of life that repeats itself endlessly and aimlessly like a spinning wheel. A Buddhist monk once wrote:

> Than nhu quang dien huu hoan vo;
> Xuan huu thinh, thu huu kno.
> Nham dam thinh suy nho bo uy.
> Thinh suy nhu lo thao bac dau kho

> Life is like a flash of light;
> Full of vigor in youth, withered in old age.
> Think about it. Life is a game of vicissitudes.
> Youth, aging are like mildew clinging to morning grasses.

Many Vietnamese believe in this Nothingness teaching of Buddhism, and they feel no attachment to life.

In Vietnamese literature, old age is considered a good and sweet sign. Usually in fairytales, the old are portrayed as kind and wise. And in poetry, old age is often associated with mother love and sweetness. A poet once compared an aged mother to the fragrance of a spring banana, to the warmth and nourishment of honey and glutinous rice, and to the sweetness of autumn sugarcane in his poem "Aged Mother":

Me gia nhu chuoi Gia Huong
nhu xoi nuoc mat, nhu duong mia lao

Aged mother is like Gia Huong banana*
Like honeyed glutinous rice, like young sugarcane.

By associating the old woman with sweet foods, the poet links her to love because, in Vietnamese culture, sweet foods mean love.

*Gia Huong is a common name for a type of very sweet and aromatic banana popular in Vietnam.

Tan Luong

In my country, the old have real value in each family as well as in society. Their role is to connect people and to make peace when conflicts arise. They are respected for their life experience. We believe that the more time people live, the more knowledge and good ideas they have. If the children in a family have problems, the first people they ask for advice are their grandparents. The old have the role of explaining conflicts and determining who is wrong. They are like lawyers in the family. They know that their children will respond to their needs because of the care they gave them in the past. In the larger society, the old act as counselors. They are considered clever in almost any activity. Usually they do not say much about their opinions but make them known. Each village has a group of old people who always stay at home but give advice to the head of the village.

In my country, old people use medicine only when they really need it. If they are sick, they use herbs first. After that, if they don't get any results, they change to prescription drugs. If they are sick enough to need prescriptions, they think they will die soon.

Dahn Chau Ho was raised in a peasant family in Vietnam. In 1988, he escaped to the United States. He studied mechanical engineering at Cal Polytechnic, san Luis Obispo.

Tan Luong formerly attended City College of San Francisco.

Aging in My Culture

Ponloeu Lao

Everything in the universe ages through time. When my dog was young, for example, it ran fast and barked very loud. Now that it is older, it runs slower and can't bark as loudly as before. Non-living things also age through time, for example, a car's engine. As it becomes old, the engine doesn't supply as much power as it used to. A star also ages through time. It starts as a hot, bright, giant star and eventually becomes a small, white dwarf. As humans age, their experiences about life accumulate, and they become more important to society. They will never stop learning until they reach death.

One thing I have learned growing up in Cambodia is that we are proud of our age. It is a sign of an ability to think critically, to make important decisions, and to have responsibilities, for example, our children. Old people are very important in our culture. They practice Buddhism constantly; therefore, they can teach young people the difference between good and bad deeds and can tell them how to perform good deeds, to show respect for the old, for example. Only old people have the patience to sit in a Buddhist temple for several hours three or four days a week.

Young people depend on the old in other ways as well. We ask them about the right time to be married. Later we ask them how to raise our children and how to keep our marriage from breaking up. An old person is so important that, even if he or she lacks education and wealth, young people must respect him or her, because we believe that the old have more life experience than any of us.

At age twenty, I am considered young in Cambodian culture, too young, in fact, to participate with the old when they are talking or eating in groups. My relationship with the old, however, is different from that of other young people; many old people I know like me and invite me to have dinner with them. If I refuse to join them, they keep on insisting, and sometimes they even grab my hand and pull me to the chair. When I am around them, I feel confident. Every old person I know is just like my parents. I need their help as much as they need mine. Every Sunday, I drive them to the temple in Berkeley. Along the way, they teach me the philosophies of Buddhism, which I want to learn very much.

Aging to me is rather exciting. I want to find what is waiting to take place in my life. What will I be like? Will I have good health and a successful career? If I have a wife and family, will we live a happy life? The only way to answer these questions and to discover what is to be discovered is through the aging process. Aging is only fair to me. I have been given life to explore the earth, and, later, as I become old, my life will be taken away form me to allow another living thing to explore the earth just as I have done.

Ponloeu Lao studied writing at City College of San Francisco.

Folktale

Annie P. Truong

This story was passed down from one generation to another, especially when people mentioned Thanh Long, a small village in mid-South Vietnam famous for its beautiful scenery. What is unusual about this village is a connection of three ponds around a little piece of land that protrudes in the center like a small island. It was named Ho Ba Be.

Once upon a time, there was a village in Thanh Long province where people lived mainly by farming. One day, an old lady was walking around the village begging for food, but the villagers ignored her. She had been walking through the village all day long begging from one house to another, but no one bothered to share any food with her or show her any compassion.

The next day, the villagers found that a little house had been built on the corner of an open meadow next to the rice field–the old lady had built her own house to live in. In order to get food, she took care of the farmers' children, but usually they gave her only leftovers.

One day, the old lady was making a fence around her little house. When she asked the villagers to help her finish it, they laughed at her. One of them said, "What valuable object can you possibly have that you think someone might want to rob your dirty little pig house? You silly old lady."

She replied, "My dear people, you do not understand. Tomorrow there will be a big storm, and together we can build a larger fence with enough space for the whole village to stay during the storm. Believe me, it will save your lives."

The villagers laughed even harder. One exclaimed, "You fool! What are you talking about? It never rains in March (in Vietnam, the rainy season starts in June). Besides, our houses made of brick are stronger than yours and will withstand any storm."

The next morning, the old lady finished the fence by herself. When the villagers brought their children to her house, she urged them to come back and stay behind the fence for the afternoon until the coming storm was over. No one listened to her. Some even threatened her, saying that if she did not stop telling nonsensical stories, they would burn her house and chase her out of the village.

When the afternoon came, huge dark clouds invaded the blue sky and covered the sun. The rain poured down so hard that it flooded the village except for the old lady's house, which was surrounded by the fence. All the people in the village were killed. The only survivors were the old lady and the children in her house. When the storm was over, a small piece of land surrounded the old lady's house. Nearby were three water ponds. Because the people of Thanh Long had shown no compassion for the poor and no respect for the elderly, they were punished for their rudeness and selfishness.

Annie P. Truong graduated from the nursing program at City College of San Francisco.

The Older, the Stronger

Kern Peng

There is a commonly used idiom in Chinese. The translation is, "The older, the stronger." It means an elder does not give up on something because of his or her age. This idiom came from the East Han Dynasty of China. A general named Ma Yuan was a knowledgeable person who had rendered outstanding service to his country. When he was over sixty, the people of Dong Ting were fighting against his country. His emperor, Guang Wu, sent an army to conquer those people, but the whole army was defeated. Knowing, this, Ma Yuan went to the emperor and recommended himself for the job of conquering the rebels. Guang Wu considered for a while and then said, "You are too old for that." But Ma Yuan insisted, "I can still ride a horse. I don't feel old." He took his weapon and jumped on a horse to prove to his emperor that he was not old. Guang Wu praised him by saying, "The older you are, the stronger you are." The emperor allowed him to lead the army, and they were victorious. Thus, the old general served his country again in his old age.

Kern Peng came to the U.S. from China as a teenager and studied at City College of San Francisco. He holds an MBA from San Francisco State University and a Ph.D. in business administration from Golden Gate University. He is currently working on another doctorate, in mechanical engineering, at Santa Clara University, where he has taught in engineering management for several years. He works for Intel. He and his wife have two daughters.

YuGong Moved the Mountains

Shi Cheng Li

In a small mountain village of northern China once lived an old man and four generations of his family. The old man, named YuGong (meaning a stupid person in Chinese) was ninety years old but still very healthy. His big family ran well under his control. A great problem for the family, however, was its isolation from other people because of the location of their house. In front of it, two mountains, named TaiHang mountain and Yellow-House mountain, cut it off from the outside world. Every day they had to go a long distance to get to the marketplace. As a result, the whole family had a hard time selling their products and buying their bread-and-butter necessities. Everyone in the family felt the inconvenience, but nobody could do anything about it.

Once day, YuGong, as the respected authority in the family, called everyone to a meeting to discuss their problem. Finally, they agreed to adopt the old man's plan to level the high mountains into a plain by chipping away at them. Then the family could go directly to the marketplace. Early the next morning, the old man led everyone in his family–the men and the women, the old and the young–to the mountains to start performing their great task. They needed to move the stones, cut the trees and dig up the mountain. At first, some of the young men wanted to give up because they lacked patience for this long-term plan of removing the mountains. But, whenever they saw the hard-working, ninety-year-old man, they were moved and gained more energy and confidence in the plan. They went to work before the sun rose and went back home after he sun set. Day by day, the whole family kept working under the leadership of the old man.

In the neighboring village lived a man who considered himself very smart. When he heard that YuGong's family was going to move those two big mountains by hand, he was surprised. In his mind, moving the mountains couldn't ever be done, by any people, using any means. Immediately he went to see how YuGong's family was faring.

"Hey, old man," he said, "this time your name really applies to what you are doing. I can't believe you are so stupid. Look, you are already ninety years old, and you should not expect to live too much longer. You will be a superman if you can move one eighth of one of the mountains by the time your last day finally comes. Is that right?" The "smart" person laughed loudly at YuGong.

"I'm no fool," replied YuGong. "You're the fool. What I am doing isn't for myself but for my children and for my children's children. We can't escape from the fact that the mountains are not going to go away by themselves. I don't want our children to face this inconvenience forever. Though I won't live to see any progress on moving the mountains, my children may, or their children, if we keep doing it. We have confidence and perseverance." he added firmly. Then he gave a big laugh.

Finally, after many, many years, YuGong's family moved the two high mountains. After that, they could go on a short path directly to the marketplace instead of walking a long distance. Human beings have vast power when they really mean to do something and keep doing it. YuGong and his family were not scared by the difficulty of moving the mountains. They meant to do it and they kept doing it. They knew that they would finally finish the work some day in the future. Although people can't create their natural environment, they can change it if they really mean to do so.

Shi Cheng (Steven) Li studied at City College of San Francisco and later at Cal Poly, San Luis Obispo, where he received a B.S. in electrical engineering. He works in Silicon Valley as a design engineer for Broadcom. He and his wife have a son.

The Jizos Wore Sedge Hats

Masako Saigo Cohen

Once upon a time, there was an old married couple. In spite of being poor, they lived a quiet, peaceful life in a snowy mountain village. On the day before New Year's, the old man said, "Tomorrow will be New Year's, but we have no money to buy mochi." Mochi was a rice cake that people ate on New Year's Day. He looked for something to sell and remembered gathering some sedge during the summer. "Let's make sedge hats and sell them in town," the old woman said.

When they had made five hats, the old man went to the nearest town in the snow. The town was very crowded with people who were shopping because there was a special market on New Year's Eve. The old man tried to sell the sedge hats in the marketplace, but no one bought any of his hats. Finally, he had to go back home without any money or mochi. As the old man walked through the withered trees of the forest, snow flakes were endlessly falling down upon him and his sedge hats. By the time he got back near his village, the wind had become stronger, and a great snowstorm was beginning. In the heavy snow, he saw six stone statues of Jizo, the guardian deity of the villagers. They were standing by the roadside deep in snow. Their heads and shoulders were covered with icy snow, and they appeared to be shivering in the cold weather.

"How miserable," the old man said to the stone statues. "You must be very cold." Then he took the heavy snow off the Jizos' heads and shoulders and put a sedge hat on each head and tied it. Since there were six Jizos, he did not have a hat for the last one. The old man took off his muffler and covered the last Jizo's head with it.

"Keep off the cold with these hats and a muffler," he said to the statues. Then he felt peaceful and hurried home. When the old man returned home, his wife burned some dead wood and built up a good fire for him to warm himself. She asked about the sedge hats, and, when the old man told her about the Jizos, she praised him, saying, "You have done a wonderful thing today." Her tender heart made him feel good, and they were very happy.

In the middle of the night, the old couple heard a distant sound calling out "Yo-ho, yo-ho," gradually approaching the village. It was the six Jizos singing, "Where is the good old man who gave sedge hats to the Jizos? Where is the good old man who made sedge hats for the Jizos?" The sound of the song was getting louder and louder and stopped in front of the old couple's house. Suddenly, there was a sound of something heavy being unloaded outside their door. The old couple anxiously drew open the door and were surprised to find lots of freshly made mochi, fish, fruit, and vegetables under the eaves. The snowstorm had stopped, and the stars were shining in the clear sky. When the old couple looked beyond the snow field, they saw the backs of six Jizos going away. The Jizos were wearing the sedge hats and the muffler and were heard singing gaily in the distance.

Masako Saigo Cohen was born in Japan and received a B.A. in painting from Jakugei University in Tokyo. Her work has been exhibited in several art shows in Japan, and painting has remained a primary focus throughout her life. In the United States, she continued her education at City College of San Francisco, where she received an A.A. degree in Fine Arts, and at San Francisco State University.

The Old Couple and Their Goat
Iraqi Folktale

Note: In Iraqi folktales, a dāmi is a half-bestial ogress who haunts the outskirts of towns. She has a liking for human flesh.

Once upon a time, there was an old couple, and they kept a goat, of which they were very fond. Their house was of clay and their door of reeds, and they and the goat lived there together.

Once day a dāmi, who lived in the desert nearby, became hungry for human blood, and she said to herself, "I will eat either that old man or that old woman!" So she went to the house and knocked at the reed door and said:

Yā bāb al qasab,	"O reed door!
Ākassar 'anak	I will break you down!
Lo ujāiz lo shwāyib bi	I will eat up your little old
ākul 'anak!	woman or your little old man!"

Now the old woman was alone in the house, and, when she heard this, she was very afraid, but the goat was listening, and she answered, "With my horns, I will butt you, and with my teeth, I will bite you!"

When the dāmi heard this, she was frightened of the goat and ran away back into the desert.

But she was still very hungry. The next day she came again and knocked at the gate. The old woman, who was alone, said, "*Minu?* Who is it?" The dāmi said,

"O reed door!
I will break you down!
I will eat up your little old woman and your little old man!"

And the goat answered, "With my horns I will butt you, and with my teeth, I will bite you!" and the dāmi was frightened and ran away.

Now as the dāmi was going along the road, whom should she meet but the old man. She said to him, "Every day I come to your house to give you some food from the Sultan's house, but your goat will not let me in!"

The old man went back and said to his old woman, "What is this? The dāmi brings us food every day from the Sultan's house, and our goat will not let her in! I shall kill the goat!"

Answered the old woman, "O, husband, is your understanding wanting? The goat stands before the door because the dāmi wants to eat us! Don't kill the goat!"

The next day it was the same. The dāmi came, and the goat would not let her in, and the dāmi complained to the old man. But after the dāmi had complained for the third time, the old man took his knife and prepared to kill the goat. The old woman cried, "O husband, do not believe the dāmi! She wants to eat us! She is hungry for our blood! Do not kill the goat!"

But the old man went to the goat and cut her throat.

The old woman wept and cried, "*Shlōn sowweyt!* What have you done!" But, as the goat was dead, she roasted some of the meat and made pācha* of the head and oddments, and the rest she put in a pot of brine.

The next day the dāmi came and cried:

"O reed door!
I will break you down!
I will eat up your little old woman and your little old man!"

And from the pot of brine a voice came from the meat, "With my horns, I will butt you, and with my teeth I will bite you!"

And the dāmi was frightened and ran away.

That night, the old man ate up the meat that was left. The next day the dāmi came before he had gone out, and she cried to the door,

"O reed door!
I will break you down!
I will eat up your little old woman and your little old man!"

And this time, there was no answer. Inside the house, the old woman said, "Now you hear for yourself! The dāmi wants to eat us!"

The old man ran off and hid in the clay oven, and the old woman rolled herself in some matting and hid in the room.

The dāmi cried again at the door and there was no answer, so she pushed with her head, and the door gave way, and she entered and wandered about the hōsh.** The old man, in his fright, let a sound escape him in the oven.

Called the dāmi:

Menu darrat?	"Who made that noise?
Al hāyit darrat?	Was it the wall?
Al bāb darrat?	Or the door?
Al bait darrat?	Or the house?"

And she wandered about looking. *Dí!* She came to the oven. She looked in the oven, and there she saw the old man!

Said she:

Menu darrat?	"Who made that noise?
Ash shāib darrat!	The old man did!
Shlōn aktalak?	How shall I kill you?"

The old man said, "Because I did not listen to my wife's advice when she asked me not to kill the goat, now you are going to eat me!"

The dāmi took him and tore him in two halves and ate him all up and returned to her lair in the desert.

As for the old woman, she brought some friends to live with her in the house, and the dāmi did not return there again.

This tale was recorded by an Englishwoman, **Lady Eleanor Stevens**, who lived in Iraq. The teller is identified as Lili, a Baghdad Christian woman. Lady Stevens published *Folk-Tales of Iraq* in London in 1931.

*Pācha is a stew made of sheep's offal, the head, and the feet.
**Hōsh is all the ground, including the yard, enclosed by the house-wall.

Annie at 109

At home, over anisette,
and a game of chess,
my wife recalls

Old Annie, who,
at 109, in the small
Dakota town my wife
is from, would bless
the children as they

came around with gifts
of wild plum jam
and lilacs embroidered
on towels and winter

scarves. Each day
Old Annie would sit
with the girl my wife
still is, and hum

through the afternoon
with games of Chinese
checkers. Now, these
years between,

as my wife maneuvers
her mate into check
for the hundredth
time, she revels

in the memory
of Annie, and her
miraculous age,

how she retained
her wonderful marbles
and never threw a game.

Tom Domek

Tom Domek is the author of several books including an upcoming guidebook from Falcon Press titled *Family Fun in the Black Hills and Badlands* and a biography, *On the Border Lines of Justice: Reverend Richard Sinner and the Sanctuary Movement.* His poetry has appeared in numerous journals. He lives with his family in Custer, South Dakota.

Promise for 65

I'm expecting my next blood next week.
Your last long gone,
you can play tennis, jog at dawn
and never stop for cramps.
Already I'm jealous.
Twenty years and ten pounds on me,
you've caught me laughing,
helpless with lust in your muscled hold,
your lips on my neck, my breasts,
like a carp nibbling.
Look out, I'm a swimmer!
In a few days I'll give you
sweet mollusk, my best years beginning
now as I gain
strength and grow
toward your irresistible age.

Jacqueline Lapidus

Jacqueline Lapidus grew up in New York City and lived in Greece and then France for many years. In France, she was active in international feminist groups. An editor, teacher, and translator who worked most recently on the latest edition of *Our Bodies, Ourselves*, she teaches the writing component of a course on medical issues and information at Harvard Extension School.

Drought

Once we said thunder
was the old man of sky snoring,
lightening was the old man
striking a match,
but now we only want him to weep
so we tell him our stories
in honest tongues.

Linda Hogan

Linda Hogan, poet, short story writer, novelist, playwright, and essayist grew up in Oklahoma. She obtained an M.A. from the University of Colorado in 1978. Often writing from a feminist perspective, Hogan has played an important role in development of Native American poetry, particularly as its relationship to environment and anti-nuclear issues. Her awards include a Guggenheim and Wordcraft Circle Writer of the Year (prose-fiction) in 1997.

Aging Is Not for Sissies

miss rosie

when I watch you
wrapped up like garbage
sitting, surrounded by the smell
of too old potato peels
or
when i watch you
in your old man's shoes
with the little toe cut out
sitting, waiting for your mind
like next week's grocery
i say
when i watch you
you wet brown bag of a woman
who used to be the best looking gal in georgia
used to be called the Georgia Rose
i stand up
through your destruction
i stand up

Lucille Clifton

Lucille Clifton writes poetry, fiction, and children's books. *Blessing the Boats: New and Selected Poems* won the 2000 National Book Award for poetry. Both *Good Woman: Poems and a Memoir 1969-1980* and *Next: New Poems* were finalists for the 1988 Pulitzer Price. Clifton is Distinguished Professor of Humanities at St. Mary's College in Maryland and a Fellow of the American Academy of Arts and Sciences.

Fierce with Reality

The King of the Tables

by Andrew McNabb

Glenn Miller's *"Blue Rain"* floats like a memory through the basement of St. Gregory's Church on Broadway. It's staticy, but it's gorgeous, and Frank can practically see young Glenn and his orchestra as if they were right there beside him, mouths blowing brass, Ray Eberle holding the mic, and Glenn's foot working it, tap-tapping the black and white tiled floor, so church-like, sealed by glossy wax and time...*Blue, blue rain, falling down my window pane* ... sings Ray, setting an elbow fat with arthritis in motion, a humped back bounding back and forth, spotted hands afloat. Frank leans against one of the thick basement poles and takes in the scene, the dozen seniors preparing the hall for the weekly soup kitchen. It had been his idea, bringing in the old phonograph, and Father Mike hadn't objected, and now look at those old bones go ... *But when you return there'll be a rainbow, after the blue, blue rain* ... Inside it's 1942 again and outside it's early spring, still chilly and blue sky New England. Frank is wearing his best cardigan sweater and gray pants. And today will be the day.

Her name is Rose Breeley and there she is, sitting next to Mary Simmons, wrapping donated cutlery in scratchy napkins. He watches her hands, so delicate, the way she takes the fork and spoon, wrapping them carefully, lovingly ... *Today, tomorrow*, sings Frank to himself, inserting his words into Glenn's song. Today, he would ask Rose to have tea, for tomorrow, at her home. His place just wasn't suitable. He'd recently moved into BonnyCrest where the slogan was "Choice," which was supposed to mean all sorts of things but when it came right down to it it just meant assisted living or unassisted. He was unassisted now but it wouldn't be that way forever. That morning he'd woken up soaked in his own urine.

56

But Rose Breeley wasn't nearly at that point yet. She was the youngest one there, just seventy and her husband had been a university professor, the famous kind, the kind who wrote books and went on news programs and Frank knew Rose was not unsuitable for that type of man–so different from him, who'd had a career selling fasteners. Frank knew she lived in a big home on Seychelles Avenue. It was the one with the giant beech tree out front imported from Europe a hundred years ago with this day in mind, when it would tower over the house, the street, and Oceanside itself, its base as thick as a small truck. She kept up that house all by herself.

… And there's a blue star, looking down asking where you are … Frank moves on, heading for the supply closet, enjoying the music and the calm, the quiet before the rush of hungry bodies through the door, when the mood would sometimes change inside. "Come on, you scattered old fuck!" one of the men had said last week to Frank when his food hadn't come out quickly enough, and Frank had pretended not to hear him. They did it differently there at St. Gregory's. Each of the churches in town took one day a week feeding the hundred and fifty mouths, but St. Gregory's was the only Catholic one and the only one to serve the men and women, not have them wait in line. Father Mike had insisted on it. But there were more mouths now for some reason and the number of servers was dwindling. Hattie had died just last week. Frank had gone to elementary school with her. She crosses his mind now, but he pushes her away. He looks out over the scene again, the bodies bumping ever-so-slightly to the music, the lightness of it all, and he thinks how it wouldn't be so bad to freeze this spot in time. So much had changed, but at least they were all together. The emptiness of his room at BonnyCrest fades as he lets his eyes go unfocused, and sweet Ray sings *… Then there'll be no more blue rain, just the sound of my heart's refrain, singing like a million bluebirds, after the blue, blue rain …*

~

Out in the back room, Frank gathers supplies, and phrases a little conversation in his head. "Look at that Rose, The King of the Tables has us working side-by-side again." He envisions her laughing sweetly, and she would reply, *"That King."* It's how it had happened last week. Frank was the one in charge of assigning servers to tables and for the last month he'd made sure to put Rose on the next table over from him. When there was down time, they would be close enough to chat. He spent all week thinking of things to say. Today, he would say, "Say, Rose, how about a cup of tea some time? Yes? How about tomorrow?"

A knock at the supply room door startles him. "Frank?"

"Yup, just getting …" He grabs two big cans of tomatoes and emerges from behind the door.

Jerry, his best friend, is standing there. He's still solid, like Frank; but he's a half a foot shorter and has weathered time a bit better. Frank has a slight limp he covers up mostly by going slowly. Frank and Jerry had been together at Dumont Elementary, and then at the high school and then right into the military together, fought at the Battle of the Bulge side-by-side. Jerry married Doris and Frank married Anne. They were both gone now, and enough time had passed that Jerry could sometimes say with a smile, "Those ladies couldn't outlast us, could they, Frankie?"

"Everyone's at the back," Jerry says now. They gather at the back every week for coffee and a bit of conversation before the doors open.

Frank brings the cans out and puts them on the nearest table. He thinks the women may be looking over and so he takes his time, looking to see if there is a spot near Rose. There is, straight across from her. As they approach the table, Jerry puts his arm around Frank and says, "Ladies, I'd like to introduce my father."

"Get outta here," says Frank, pulling away, and the ladies laugh.

Jerry was the comic in their act of comedian and straight man, but Frank could have killed Jerry just now. He looks to Rose. She's smiling. No damage done.

"Great music, Frank," says Winnie, and the others agree. Winnie is flagged by her husband, Jim, who never leaves her side. "You know, it was that very song that we used to dance to at Parlor night?" she says to Jim.

"No, it wasn't," says Jim. "It was *Summer, Summer*. That was our song."

"Was it?" says Winnie. "I don't remember."

"Ahh," says Jim, waving a hand.

"Hey, Frank, did you see that Charlie O'Neill died?" says Winnie.

"Charlie?" says Frank, taking a moment to remember who Charlie O'Neill was.

Jerry pipes in, "They say that more World War II veterans die each day now than they did during the war." He looks proud of himself for the knowledge, and that time was tougher than the Germans and the Japs had been.

"Can't run from time," says Winnie. That brings a few nods.

The conversation carries on that way for a while. Frank is quiet and he knows the longer he goes, the harder it will be to say something. "It was 1942," interjects Frank.

"What was?" says Jerry.

"This song. The year was 1942. Do you remember, Jer? We took a cargo plane back from France and this was playing in the terminal in New York when we landed."

Jerry looks puzzled. "I think so," he says.

"I just thought it might be fun," says Frank. "Bringing in the old phonograph. You like the song, Rose?"

"I do," says Rose.

"*Bringing in the back way, bringing in the front way,*" sings Winnie, and Jim jumps in, right along beside her.

But Jerry interrupts. "Ope, shhh everybody ... Ladler approaching." That brings a few laughs. Old Ry has just emerged from the kitchen. Ry and Mary–and Hattie until she died–worked in the kitchen as ladlers. In the social strata, ladlers were one step up from hungry mouth and two steps down from server. It was a job for the infirm; they didn't have to move.

"Hey, Ry, how goes it?" says Jerry.

"Fine," says Ry, giving a sideways glance. He's dressed in an old suit and his mouth hangs open slightly. He sits down with an oomph.

They go back to their conversation. Frank looks over at Rose every so often and manages to get in a word now and then. So close to her now, he's losing his nerve for later. He wonders if he'll be able to ask her, and what she'll say. She's not even Catholic. But then she says to him, "So, Frank, where does the King of the Tables have me working today?"

Frank is elated, and looks at his pad as if he didn't already know, and says, "He's got you on two, Rose. And he's got me on one." He smiles and winks.

"*That King,*" she says.

Everyone else is engaged in conversation and Frank doesn't think he can wait. "Say, Rose?"

"Yep?"

But Father Mike appears at the basement steps, and Jerry says, "Speaking of Fathers."

"Bread's here!" calls Father Mike to the back, and Jerry taps Frank on the arm. "Bread's here," he says.

They get up and head out front together, where Father Mike is waiting with the back of the church truck filled up.

~

It's crisp outside, and Frank wishes he'd put on his coat. The line is beginning to fill in, and he glances over to see if the drunk who'd insulted him last week is there. No sign of him just yet. As they approach the truck, Father Mike says, "Hey, boys. What's for lunch?"

"Lasagna," says Jerry.

"Lasagna, lasagna," replies Father Mike, and Frank just smiles and heads for the bread. Frank never knows what to say around Father Mike, who is a young priest and one who rarely wears his Roman collar; and all of a sudden on Sunday you greet your neighbor before mass begins, and hold hands during the Our Father, and for some reason there is no bell ringing at consecration time.

Jerry grabs a few bags stuffed with day old bread and heads inside. When Frank goes to reach for some himself, Father Mike says, "Frank, I've been meaning to talk to you about something."

Though much had changed about Frank—his sinew now stretched past its tension, his hair just a rectangular silver strip at the back of his head—his eyes have maintained their savage blue, and he looks at Father Mike through them now, for what this might be about.

"Frank, I saw what was happening last week during the meal."

"Rose?" says Frank.

"Excuse me?" replies Father Mike.

Frank shuts up.

Father Mike continues, "That man. The way he said something to you."

"Oh, that," says Frank. "It's not a big deal."

"Well, maybe not, Frank." Father Mike brushes his sweater with his hand, picking away at a stray lint ball. "It's just that we're in a rush down there at meal time. We serve fifty more meals a day now than we did this time last year. We need those meals out and to the table not just so the clients can get their meals quickly, but so they can leave and open their seat for the people waiting." He signs and looks Frank in the eye. "And that man, he's unstable, Frank. Think about the liability we'd have if something were to happen to you."

Frank feels the heat going to his face. His big hands come together, squeeze tightly.

"So we'd like you on ladling duty now, as opposed to working the tables. We'll start with that today."

"No, no, Father. I don't think that's a good idea."

Father Mike puts his hand on Frank's big shoulder. "I thought you might say so, Frank. But it's all God's work."

Frank thinks of Rose. "No, Father, you don't understand."

"I'm going to take your table today, Frank. Until we get someone else to fill it."

Frank is nearly speechless; he tries to keep the conversation going any way he can. "I'd like to play the music through lunch if I could."

Father Mike smiles. "I don't know if that would be appropriate, Frank. Maybe we can discuss it at the meeting next week."

~

Back inside, Frank floats ambivalently between the table he'd assigned himself to cover and the kitchen, where the real boss had put him. The last half hour has been a blur of potential options. He'd disappear for a while, wandering back to the supply room. Looking into a big box of pasta, he'd yelled, "You're like a Goddamn Protestant minister!" He'd opened and closed his fists. "I was a Marine!"

His anger had brought him back out into the hall, but he was lost once he saw everybody going about their business.

Jerry approaches him now and says, "You don't look so good, Frank. What was that about with Father?"

"Oh," says Frank. "Just a," he stops, clenches his jaw. "That goddamn bum."

"Was it about that creep from last week?"

Frank looks up from the floor and into Jerry's eyes. "No … nope."

"Okay, Frankie, whatever you say."

They stand there for a moment, silent. Frank sees Jerry look at the clock. It is just a few minutes before the doors will open. "Come on, they're just about ready to beat down the doors," says Frank and he turns and goes to the serving station where the servers are gathering their trays. Frank looks to Rose, so carefree, banging the tray against her leg like a schoolgirl. He considers up and leaving. But where would Mondays be spent?

Instead of following Jerry, Frank goes to the back entrance to the kitchen. Inside, he takes Hattie's old spot between Ry and Joan. They don't say anything about his being there, as if it is just as natural as could be. "Frank, you're on fruit cup," says old Ry, and he hands Frank a ladle.

~

In the tray in front of him is an assortment of cherries, pears, tangerines and grapes. He stares into it, and feels himself shriveling. His eyes move to the hand that holds the ladle. It looks like someone else's.

Out of the corner of his eye, he sees the servers lined up at the entrance to the kitchen. He stares straight ahead. But that will only make it worse so he forces himself to look over. There's Winnie, Jim, Jerry. Thank God no Rose. Yet. He smiles. "Hey, ho," he says. "Get your fruit cup." He laughs foolishly.

The doors to the outside open and the sound of feet rushing down the stairs fill the kitchen, trampling his will. He knows there won't be tea. But where did it go? Out with the years. This wasn't how he'd lived his life. It didn't mean he had to take it. The servers move through the line. There's a glimpse of Rose's red blouse. And Father Mike.

And all of a sudden, it's 1942 again. Frank jumps out from behind the serving table and rushes out into the hall. A few servers yell for him to stop. "He's going for him!" yells Jerry. But before anyone can get to him, Frank's got old Glenn and his boys pump-pumping at full blast, the hall is nearly shaking with the sound … *At last my love has come along, my lonely days are over, and life is like a song, the skies above are …*

"Frankie!" calls Jerry.

But Frank was gone, smiling like a child as he disappears up the stairs and out into the blue sky sunshine.

Andrew McNabb lives with his wife and two children in Portland, Maine. His stories have been published in *New Delta Review, Potomac Review, Many Mountains Moving* and other journals. He is currently at work on a story collection.

A Day with Dad

Lynn Scott

"Carolyn, Carolyn, Carolyn, help, help, help, help, Carolyn, Carolyn …" The voice drums at me through the intercom, piercing my drugged sleep, making raw my already-jangled nerves.

"Oh, God, help me." Like an echo of my father's refrain, I beseech some Being out beyond me. "How much more can I take, dear God?"

I am already on my downstairs, slippers and robe hastily gathered against the cold of this draughty New England Victorian house. Midstairs, I hear his voice and the echo of it from the intercom above me: "Help, help, help."

"How *can* an eighty-nine-year old, sick and awake half the night, have the strength to keep that yawling up?" I am talking out loud, my anger rising.

"All right, Dad. I'm here. Stop yelling," I yell over his steady cries.

"Well, dammit, where have you been? I made a mess, and I have been lying in it for hours." His tone and the fierce blue eyes above his long white beard reveal the tough old German behind the former pathetic cries.

"No you *haven't.* Just two hours ago I was here, and you were all cleaned up. It is barely dawn, and I am *tired.*"

"Get me up. I want a cup of coffee."

Wearily, I gather hot water, soap, towel, diaper, and a sheet. My anger softens as I pull back the blankets and expose the frail body that looks like pictures I have seen of men in concentration camps. His catheter tube pokes out from his penis and drapes across his leg to the bag on the floor. Sadness rises now, as quickly as my anger. Where is my strong daddy whose male parts I only imagined and never wanted to know so intimately, whose hands looked so beautiful to me, even when he used them to tease and roughouse? Where is the daddy who called me his darling daughter and was so generous and safe in my teen years?

"What are you waiting for?" His querulous demands break through my reverie, and I take up the matter at hand—the fecal matter at hand. How *does* he produce so much when he eats so little?

"Oh, Dad, you are shitty from one end to the other. Now be patient. I have to get the dirty sheet out from under you. Help me. Roll on your right side."

"Oh, I can't, I can't. I'm falling off the bed."

Patiently now, recalling our reversed roles, recalling all the times in my young past when tragedies would send me scurrying to his waiting arms, where I could weep without reproach, I assure him that I have him, and he will not fall. I wrestle the dirty sheet out and wash his back, then slip a clean sheet under him before turning him over to the other side. Again he fears a fall. Again I assure him that I have him securely.

At last! Diaper and pants are on. I button his shirt, put his socks over the ugly purple-discolored ankles, swollen tautly. I pull up the wheelchair, talking to myself: "Remember to lock the wheels, Lynn."

He is dead weight despite his frail look, and errors in the past have landed us both on the floor. It is almost impossible for me, alone, to get him up and into a chair.

Now as I move him toward the wheelchair, I hear the fatal sound–a fart and a swish. The brown ooze dribbles down his pant legs and into his socks and slippers.

"Oh, Dad, *no!*"

He giggles, then laughs out loud as I return his frame to the bed. I have a choice. I can be miserable at the prospect of starting over, or I can join him in his rare belly laugh and turn it into a cosmic joke. I try the second route.

"Man, *you are one steady shitter.* Oh, God, it is *everywhere*! I have to start *all over.*"

He laughs heartily, and somehow we draw closer.

He is up, clean, beard and hair brushed neatly, and enjoying his bacon, eggs, and coffee. At last, a break for me. I have the washer doing his daily load. Today it will have to run a second time to keep him in clothes. I will have to scrub his room completely, but it can wait until the winter sun warms the kitchen porch a bit. Thank goodness for that silly narrow-windowed space that heats up enough to air things despite the deep winter.

Dad dozes all morning in his big wing chair. I check on him every so often, but the time is mine. I spend it upstairs in my sunny-windowed bedroom. Here, at my desk, I work on my book, an ambitious project about women's relationships, which seem so distant to me now. Or I pour my feelings into an ongoing journal, or I read the constant companions of these days of isolation and internal ferment: Buber and Frankl, Sarton and Griffin, Etty Hillesum, my soul sister, who penned a journal of transformation while the Nazi solution for Holland closed in around her. These are the spirits with whom I converse.

Sometimes Dad says, "Carolyn, give me a little ice cream, will you?" or, "Give me a glass of vichy," as though I am sitting by his side. The intercom delivers his requests, and I slip down the back stairs to do his bidding.

At eleven, the Meals-on-Wheels woman arrives, and I shift from the altered state I am in with my books and my thoughts. Once again, the choice. Feeling so peaceful among them, I resist the call to that world below. Sometimes I damn well want to just sit here in my misery, wallowing in my losses: my lover, my career, my wonderful sacred hill in Maine, two dear friends who died this year, my son in terrible trouble, and my life as I might like to live it.

But today, the sun shines inspiringly on the new snow, and Dad and I *did* have that crazy sharing this morning, and I have just had three lovely hours to myself. I greet the woman with Dad's lunch cheerily and fix his tray before him. He likes this meal, and he digs in like a child, without waiting for the niceties of napkin or knife.

⌢

Noontime each day is swim and errands time for me. Sometimes Dad will snort, "Act your age!" when I announce that I am leaving for two hours to swim.

"Whatta ya mean, act my age?" I would get indignant, until I realized that he gets frightened to see me go off, wants me to be his age, stay with him, grown toward death in companionship.

I *do* want to go away, often. I hunger to be with my delicious new grandboy, Nicholas, one hundred miles away. Being Nana is like falling in love at sixteen. My heart hurts not to be able to hop into my car anytime and rush to be with him. It is all so askew. Instead of changing his darling diaper and wiping *his* little bottom, I am here, taking care of this overgrown baby.

Today I will stop at the Respite Care office and arrange a few days away. It is complicated. I have to find friends willing to be with Dad between official visits from respite workers. But it is worth even dealing with the noxious woman at Respite. Bonnie is her name. She looks attractive–about thirty-five, slim, and a swimmer like me. Her smile is pretty, but I am never warmed by it. On the contrary, I often feel chastised by her bureaucratic zeal and disapproval of my unorthodox style.

"Now, Lynn, you must give me the exact time of your arrival back from New York and a complete schedule and telephone list of those covering your father between our visits. And I want your telephone number in New York." (Smile.)

"Bonnie, my friends are very busy but are totally responsible to work out a schedule that won't leave my father alone. Your worker finishes at 8:00 p.m. You don't have to worry after that. I will tend to his overnight care."

"No, Lynn. That is not sufficient. (Smile.) For our records, we need these forms filled out completely, and I want to know what hour you plan to return."

Never as a teenager out in my father's car was I subjected to such scrutiny! Here I am, more than twenty years older than this woman, choosing to keep my father home with me, and she acts as though she cannot trust me to care for him properly. I feel my face redden, my heart shrink into a hard lump, and I know if I fall into the teenage rebel role, I will have played right into her hands.

"Thank you, Bonnie. I will mail the form back to you right away."

I drive hard to the pool, throw myself in and swim vigorously until my anger is replaced with dreams of seeing my little Nick soon.

⌣

Following Dad's long afternoon nap, I set him up with the television and a glass of port or sherry. He used to be a big drinker, but interest in drink, like almost everything else, has dwindled to this occasional evening libation. I do not allow myself free time now as I do in the morning. I feel I must offer him my company. We used to watch shows together, occasionally commenting on a performance, but, lately, he dozes the endless evenings away. This is the lonely time, when I long for someone to share the day with me. I often sit watching him, thinking of the inexorable changes that brought us to tonight, where the balance has shifted, and child has become parent.

The little changes came first—relocating him from his Florida retirement to Maine so I could watch out for him, taking over his finances when mother died. Before I could get him up from Florida, in his grief at losing his wife of almost fifty years, he had made an active campaign to replace her. First he asked each of her sisters to move in with him, which simply infuriated them. They were even more incensed when he widened his search to include all my mother's friends. Finally, he sought a wife through the personal column of the local paper. I grin even now as I remember discovering a long list of women's names and numbers in his bedside table. Next to each were notations "too young," "too old," "wants money," on down the list. At first he denied he had advertised, but I manipulated him a bit by saying, "You know, Dad, once when I was lonely, I put an ad in the papers, and I heard from thirty-five guys."

"Piker," he responded so quickly that he took me by surprise. "I heard from seventy-five women." And he admitted none were suitable.

I said a small prayer to my long-suffering mother. "It's really a compliment, Mom. He loved being with you so much that he is trying to replicate that."

Sometimes I wish he had found someone. He might have lived these ten years more fully. Then again, who would care for an old man without money and so set in his ways? Not many old women, or young ones for that matter, cared to nurse a spoiled old man. I flash on the first time I was faced with cutting his toenails. I had to push down my revulsion and fear that I would hurt him. I drew back from taking over his shaving for the same feelings and talked him into the first beard of his life.

The change from the daddy to obey when he barked out orders to his making his needs felt in gentler ways had no clear boundary but a slow eroding of our roles as I had to hold the line on his spending, insist that he change his clothes more often, or institute a healthier diet than ice cream and cake.

Somewhere before these changes came a period of about six months when he mothered me in his eighty-seventh year. I would arrive at his door, tired and hungry from my city job, and he would cook me and old-fashioned German meal—meat, potatoes, and a vegetable all cooked together in a stew—recipes he had picked up by osmosis from his mother seventy years before. I would be served a glass of wine and dinner, with my feet up on his footstool, and feel cherished by his simple attentions.

Someone had once called him a "rough diamond." I had resented it at the time, but I could see it now. A man, raised to be a gentleman by his comfortable immigrant parents, whose boundless sexual energy and irrepressible boyish charm made him a difficult husband and a complex father. We loved his spontaneous decisions to head to the beach at midnight or to rush out for ice cream most any weekday evening, but we knew, too, that he could suddenly explode into a tantrum that was short-lived but frightening. My brothers felt its effects more than I, and, if I saw my mother downcast, I would stand up and outshout him, then run to my room weeping.

Tonight I have folded his huge laundry, remade his bed, and sewn buttons on his shirt. Now I get to color. Yes, I am not even embarrassed to say that I color. I have lovely adult coloring books: Mandalas and intricate clothing of past ages and designs that stretch my creativity a bit. All that is required is the muscle of my hand and the selection of the suitable magic marker. My mind stills, time moves.

At 10:00 or 11:00 p.m., Dad and I do our dance once again. We must look from the outside as if we dance. I pull him to his feet, arms totally around him, and we swivel to the wheelchair. He sits, I push him to his bedside, and again we dance. But at this juncture, I first pull down his pants before he can sit down. How must that look from outside his window? All his clothes come off, and the nightshirt is maneuvered down and under his body. The tube must be placed so he can turn without discomfort, and a diaper attached around him to at least stem the flow of the inexorable ooze.

He wants water on the bedside table, though I know he will call me anyway because he never can find it in the night. I don't wind the clock by his bed anymore. He objected to that at first. Funny how we hang onto bits and pieces of control even when they have no relevance. I tuck him in and turn out the light.

"Good night, Dad. Have a good sleep."

Tonight he catches me off guard.

"Good night, daughter. I love you."

Lynn Scott's stories and memoirs come from her rich experience as a counselor, group leader, and aide to seniors. A contributor to *Ourselves Growing Older*, she has won awards from the Jack London Conference of the California Writing Club. Her book *A Joyful Encounter: My Mother, My Alzheimer's Clients, and Me* was published in 2005.

There She Goes

Adair Lara

When we went with Lucille to look at her new retirement home, she made the man take us up to the roof garden on the twenty-fourth floor so she could calculate the drop to the street. Tiny and hunched, her wisps of grey hair lifting in the breeze across the solarium roof, she steadied herself with one freckled hand on the retirement home man's sleeve and, peering over the railing, said, "That ought to do it."

I was shocked, standing up there staring down at the sidewalk as if we were discussing where to set out the zinnias. But that was Lucille for you. Once she said, "When you get the news that I'm gone, just pour a drink, clink glasses, and say, "Well, there she goes."

She hadn't meant to be alive at eighty-three. Being an old woman was not her style. Her style, all of her life, was to sail around the world and to buy real estate, and then con other people into managing it for a pittance. It was to have many husbands but no children, to ignore the letters that came from her tedious family in southern California, to dine in expensive restaurants and call everyone darling and honey, to drink and smoke as if there were no tomorrow because tomorrow was old age, which was unthinkable.

Yet it had arrived. When I met Lucille, she was grey and shaky, in constant pain from an inoperable back condition, and pissed off to find herself still alive.

My husband, Jim, and I met her through our roommate, Mason, a tall, thin banker in his fifties with thinning blond hair and size fourteen feet that he warmed in the oven on chilly mornings. We all lived in a large Victorian in San Francisco. Jim and I were newly married and had a baby on the way.

Mason often invited Lucille over for dinner. She always arrived wrapped to her eartips in her mink stole, though we had heated the two stories to get ready for her. Mason, who had fetched her from the retirement home, would ring the doorbell to call Jim down, and together they would boost Lucille up the two flights of steep stairs.

The rest of us—I and whoever was over for dinner that night—would wait by the mail table, and eventually her little grey head would appear at the top of the stairs. She would stop panting and look around, getting her breath, then say, "So. Who do I have to f___ to get a drink around here?"

Although, at such times, she was decidedly un-auntlike, even I always thought that Lucille was Mason's mother's sister. That was the way they chose to explain their odd friendship. They weren't related at all—they had simply been playing bridge, drinking vodka and interfering in each other's lives for thirty years.

When they met, over bridge one day, I think, he was a brilliant but unschooled kid from Mississippi, without the wit even to know that he was gay until Lucille pointed it out to him one day over a game of Russian Banque. She was a rake of fifty, with a jar of olives in the fridge and an expensive apartment filled with the debris of five marriages, the latest to an aging golf pro. She liked to kick off dinner party conversation by saying, "Well, when I was a whore in Montana …"

Mason and Lucille were two of a kind, scorning conventional ties, or seeming to. On holidays, he would call her up and say, "Merry Christmas, Luce. Did you get my card and the gift?" And Lucille would say, "Yes, it was lovely, as always. And you got mine, of course?" "Yes, the shirts were perfect. You're a dear."—except that, of course, neither of them sent the other a thing.

Something happened to the friendship, though, as Lucille grew older and more demanding. She would slowly eat a slice of the leg of lamb Mason cooked and complain that he had forced her to leave San Diego, where she had been perfectly happy drinking vodka by the pool and teaching the gay Mexican houseboy to play bridge.

Mason would smile lightly, reminding her that she had taken to drinking more and would bang into walls at night when she got up. He did not bring up the fact that she had not only several times dropped lit cigarettes into the folds of the flimsy peignoirs she constantly wore but had made two clumsy attempts at suicide, once with pills and once in the bath. A small fire in her poolside apartment made Mason realize that she could not be left alone anymore and forced him to bring her to the Bay Area.

Her lack of gratitude for this and a thousand other services—rich as she was, Lucille would make him drive forty miles to buy her an electric blanket on sale, and then complain about the color—convinced us that they had some unspoken deal. She would abuse the friendship as much as she liked, force him to be nursemaid and errand boy and accountant and chauffeur, and he would get all her money. Except that Mason didn't care about it. If the money had played the smallest part in his attentions to her, he would not have gotten mad the way he did.

No one knew exactly what the issue was when they had their last fight, except that it was almost certainly something she said to him, probably in front of other people.

When nothing anybody said would induce Mason to call Lucille, or vice versa, Jim and I started to visit her, bringing little gifts of jam and ripe bananas, and boxes of Uncle Sam cereal for her chronic constipation. She lived in Oakland, in an elegant highrise retirement home run by Episcopalians. It was the only place Mason could find that allowed residents to smoke and drink in their rooms.

Residents were encouraged to take their meals in the dining room, but Lucille didn't want to. Old people made her nervous, and she gave them a wide berth, preferring her solitary room on the fifteenth floor. It was bare except for the few possessions she had elected to keep–a huge dictionary on an iron stand, a shelf of books, a hideous circular rug she had knitted out of her old sweaters, and a case of vodka under the sink.

The traveling, the money, the thousand witty remarks tossed off over the glittering silverware, a case of vodka, and a rug made out of old sweaters– she had smoked and drunk and flirted right up to the end, and now she was tired and wanted to leave the party. Her friends, all except Mason, had already left.

I didn't blame her. I once saw Lucille struggle for a full minute just to light her cigarette, the flame from the lighter dancing in her shaking hand, and thought: Why not? Why not just fly off the twenty-fourth floor? Also, I was young and, therefore, callous. Lucille wanted to die. Well, that's what old people were supposed to do.

That was in the beginning. Toward the end, and afterwards, I realized that she had changed forever the way I thought of old people and the way I thought of myself. I had thought of them as different from me, while they were only older. If old age could happen to her, it could happen to anybody. Even to me.

Even her energetic plans for suicide impressed me. She liked to control everything in her life, right down to her exit from it.

We were always braced to hear that she had done it—made her swan dive off the twenty-fourth floor, but months and then years went by, and Lucille lived on. She stopped going downstairs for meals and almost never left her room. Mason didn't call her. It seemed, from the outside, like a particularly stupid contest of wills, but it evidently gave them satisfaction, as they kept it up.

She spent her days in her lime-green Morris chair, chilled glass in hand, reading film biographies and, several times a day, calling up that "conniving bastard" who managed her properties. We brought her the baby when it was born, stripping off her diapers in that overheated room, and gave her to Lucille to hold, standing close lest she teeter over even from that slight weight. "Never get old," she told the baby. "It's no fun."

Jim and I saw less and less of her. We had a second baby, Patrick, and moved forty miles north to a house in the country. Weeks went by before we could get down to Oakland.

The phone call came in the middle of Patrick's first birthday party, when all the babies were plopped down on the deck wearing brightly colored toy sunglasses. Lucille was dead. She had climbed into the tub with half a bottle of vodka and a razor blade and escaped her old body at last in a crimson bath.

When the birthday party was over and we had gathered up all the wrapping paper, Jim and I got a sitter and walked down to the local bar. Feeling sheepish, but having promised, we ordered vodka and clinked glasses, saying, "There she goes."

When the will was read, we learned that our children were getting bonds for their education, and we were getting the rug. She made several other bequests, to housekeepers and other children of friends, but Mason's name was not mentioned.

Adair Lara was a columnist for the San Francisco Chronicle from 1989 to 2002. In 1990, she won the Associated Press award for best California columnist. She lives with her husband and two children. Lara has written a memoir, *Hold Me Close, Let Me Go*.

Senior Citizen Trio

They carry their words into the activity room,
scrubbed air, four walls bare of decorations,
no grace—but theirs. On sidewalk gray
January days, three students warm themselves
with coffee, survivors' smiles, and once-upon-
a-time Depression tales of empty pockets,
dinners of meat and potatoes, without the meat.

They read to one another, hands and words tremble
a bit, and then the catch in the throat, his tears
surprising them, and him. His apologies magnified
by hearing aids.

"I never thought I'd cry about it," he says.
"I was twelve then, so long ago, skinny kid
selling newspapers on a cold corner,
and Nini, my Italian friend, invited me
into his loud house. His family laughed at my
thin face, wedged me between thick shoulders
at the crowded table, gave me wine, a nickname,
spaghetti. At my Lutheran house, we never
drank, and we frowned at strangers."

He laughs, but his body cries again.
He apologizes, reads his last sentence,
"Thank God," but his body cries again,
"for Italians."

The two women know all about tears.
"Vell," says Helen who came from Hungary,
at forty, peeled grapes into fruit cocktail
while she learned English, "Vell," she says,
"You vere lucky."

Marty, one of eleven children who never saw
her mother's face, who brings the picture
of the daughter she buried last year, says,
"We won't live forever, ya know.
It's good to save the stories."

Pat Mora

Pat Mora is an award-winning author of poetry, nonfiction, children's books, and the memoir *House of Houses*. Her honors include an NEA poetry fellowship and the University of Texas at El Paso Distinguished Award for 2004. She is currently a visiting professor at the University of New Mexico. She lives in Santa Fe and is the mother of three grown children.

Old Age

Paul Moran

I look in my mirror. The face looking back at me is unsmiling, the hair white and slightly disheveled. The eyes resemble the eyes of the elderly Picasso posing for one of his photographs. At the same time, they suggest someone who has recently been awakened from sleep by some nightmare of terror but has almost persuaded himself that the incident was only a harmless dream. The face is puffy and deeply lined. With dismay, I notice unsightly folds and bulges in my neck and arms. The apparition reminds me of an elderly aunt of mine who saw her reflection in a mirror and said, "That is not I." Denial becomes automatic when we are confronted with the malevolence of the changes time has wrought on our bodies and our faces. "How," I ask myself, "will it be possible for anyone to like this ugly reality that is me?" My depressing appearance is not the result of dissipation. I have a lifestyle equal in asceticism to that of any monk.

Behind the image in the looking glass, I think I can see the distorted, ugly face of death. The ghoulish figure is rapidly winking and grimacing, beckoning to me in what appears to be an effort to seem friendly and sympathetic. The result is to make the vision more repellent than ever.

In front of the mirror, I try to vanquish the specter by thinking of the words of Sir Thomas Browne, "We tearme sleepe a death, and yet it is waking that kills us, and destroyed those spirits which are the house of life. 'Tis indeed a part of life that best expresseth death."

What have I done to end up this way, living the life of a recluse, avoiding contact with neighbors, venturing out only in daylight to go to food markets, or to doctors' offices, or perhaps to a movie. Reality seems a bitter mockery of Robert Browning's lines that I memorized long ago in high school:

> "Grow old along with me!
> the best is yet to be,
> The last of life, for which the first was made."

I believe I was fated by genetic predisposition to spend my time on earth in exactly the way I have.

Entering my kitchen, I swallow a pill to help control my high blood pressure. I will take another similar pill at bedtime, together with two aspirin to prevent the formation of blood clots.

I pause to look out the kitchen window at my back yard. It is winter, but I imagine the way the yard will appear in midsummer. The whole area will, as usual, be suffering from drought. The day lilies that I planted several years ago will be struggling to bloom despite the double handicap of poor soil and heavy shade. The tomato plants, carefully placed in the sunniest part of the yard, are wilted and appear to be suffering from various diseases. I have decided that this will be my last year for these unproductive plants.

Only the night-blooming cereus appears to be thriving. No wonder! These plants, in large pots, are frequently watered and fertilized and hauled in and out of the basement every autumn and spring so as to shelter them from the rigors of a Maryland winter. The flowers, which appear about ten o'clock on late summer nights, are very large and handsome. The blooms wither and fade by morning, suggesting to the thoughtful observer the brevity of human life. This characteristic of the plant, as well as the penetrating perfume of its flowers, would seem to make it ideal for funerals. When the last mourner has left the funeral home, he may be comforted by the thought that the deceased is not left entirely alone but is attended throughout the long night be the gorgeous white blooms that most appropriately close up and fade at the first hint of dawn's arrival. My garden, then, brings forth in me images of death and decay, even in the height of summer.

I am a seventy-two-year-old white male, a retired United States government worker currently living alone in a dilapidated house that was purchased twenty-nine years ago. A widower for the last eleven years, I am also the survivor of two strokes and the long-term possessor of two diseases that, in combination, are considered by experts to dramatically reduce life expectancy: high blood pressure and diabetes. The hypertension is controlled by medication; the diabetes by a diet that omits all sweets and sugars. The diabetes, while I am aware of its very real menace, allows me to have regular foot care paid by Medicare. For medical insurance, I have both parts of Medicare and Blue Cross, which seems to adequately cover my needs. I live in a Maryland suburb of Washington, D.C., and I do not now, nor have I ever, owned a car. I see doctors and a dentist on a regular basis, and I do not smoke or drink.

In 1964, I was operated on for appendicitis. The night before I was to be discharged from the hospital, a blood clot that had formed in my left leg broke off and went to my lung. I came very close to death. I recovered but with impaired circulation in the injured leg. "An unfortunate accident," the attending physician told me. From that day to this, I have daily wrapped my defective leg in a four-inch Ace bandage, paying particular attention to a severely reddened area at the ankle that is perpetually threatening to leak a gangrenous fluid into my protective bandage. "Stasis dermatitus," the doctor writes on the bill prepared for the insurance company, which means an inflammation of the skin caused by a slowing of the current of circulating blood in my left leg.

Bizarrely, I regard the two strokes I suffered as badges of honor, the almost invisible wounds I bear as I walk seemingly by deliberate choice, a stranger among strangers.

My first stroke left me with aphasia, which means I have problems with speech and language. It also left me with gaps in my short-term memory. Most of the new facts I learn today will have been forgotten by tomorrow. The speech therapist who worked with me for a while discovered that I couldn't explain the meaning of simple proverbs like "A stitch in time saves nine," and "People who live in glass houses shouldn't throw stones," and the accumulation of data like these aid in locating the area of the brain that has been injured. A curious defect that is also the result of this stroke is that I may think of something, for instance, what I'm writing right now, and, while I'm thinking about it, I can almost visualize it creeping away, a long white thread of thought gradually disappearing in the far reaches of my brain until it is completely gone, and my mind is a blank space, empty. Experience has taught me that my original concept will, after a brief pause, return, my feelings of frustration will gradually recede, and I can once more pick up where I left off.

My second stroke left me with a minor difficulty with walking. I now journey down the street with the characteristic, rather uncertain gait of the stroke victim. I'm wary of anyone seeking directions because I may, due to incorrect signals from my injured brain, give the stranger erroneous information.

The dominant influence in my life, responsible for my excessive fondness for solitude, has been a fear of people. Often this trait is called shyness, but shyness seems such an inadequate word to describe the utter desolation of the condition. Because of it, I feel that, one by one, the young men and women of my youth eluded me, their virtues to be forever unknown, their subsequent fates destined to be always a mystery to me. Like actors at the conclusion of some films, I saw them recede down silent streets and disappear forever into the distance. Even today, the memory of youthful acquaintances ignored and opportunities for friendships squandered, troubles me.

Famous persons have appeared on television and, despite the public nature of their occupations and their amazing success at the professions, confess to being fundamentally shy. Their shyness is not mine. My shyness is injurious to every aspect of my being. It has led me, from my earliest days until now, to avoid, if at all possible, every group contact, including gatherings of church goers, veterans, political enthusiasts, senior citizens, and those organized for civic betterment. I believe it has deprived me of free will and is at least partially responsible for my loss of religious faith. It may also be the reason I have never owned a car or, indeed, never learned to drive one.

The only place where I was occasionally forced to confront my social inadequacy was at my work. There I would sometimes find it necessary to attend meetings where I would leave an entire group of people bewildered by my behavior to them, which seemed to speak unnecessarily of alienation and animosity. How, some of them must have wondered, did a person so ill-equipped to deal with people and society, pass successfully through the successive stages of the American educational system? The primary and secondary schools I attended made spasmodic efforts to redeem me. Would everyone flee from me because of a defect that I felt sure was in my very genes? Fortunately, the future was not to be quite so bleak for me. I managed to survive in life despite my handicap by combining a cautious cunning with extreme timidity.

Finally, at last, I saw an article by Christine Russell in the *Washington Post* for January 5, 1982, in which a Harvard researcher, Dr. Jerome Kagan, suggested that shyness may be genetically determined. "Shyness is one of the more permanent temperamental qualities," Dr. Kagan is quoted as saying, adding, "As adults they (the genetically shy) choose less traditional masculine vocations and are less likely to be good at things such as athletics." Later I read in the *New York Times* that two independent researchers confirmed Dr. Kagan's findings that shyness has a hereditary basis. The neighbors are friendly or, at least, try to be to me. True to my genetic inheritance, I meet all their overtures with a frozen formality, or else, equally unwelcome to them, an embarrassed attempt at joviality that ends up in failure. I retreat from all these encounters temporarily discouraged and unhappy. Eventually, they too seem intent on avoiding me. Their behavior reminds me of a line from a movie I saw when I was a sophomore in college in 1936: "Those who live to themselves will be left to themselves."

To obtain groceries, I use the buses of the Washington Area Transit Authority, taking advantage of their senior citizen discount fares of thirty cents per ride. On my return trip, seated with my three or four grocery bags on the nearest available seat to the exit, I despondently speculate on why, time after time, I am the only elderly person on the bus who finds it necessary to carry food home in this manner. My fellow passengers are predominately young. They are also mainly black, Spanish speaking, or Asian. Occasionally, there is an elderly person on the bus, usually a woman, but she is carrying a single small bag of purchases from a department store that painfully contrasts with the full bags I am holding.

Like the many painters who include human skulls in their still-life studies, the elderly today are constantly surrounded by memento mori. Is the slight tremor that I detect in my hand the precursor of Parkinson's disease? Without thinking, I place my hand on my forehead so that my thumb rests on the vein at the side of my head. I can feel the pulsations of my heart then, still busily at work measuring out the number of my allotted days on earth. I feel dismay at the thin, fragile line that separates life from death.

Once more I look through my kitchen window at the scene outside. It is March and a cold, bleak day. In my yard are three tall oak trees and a somewhat smaller hickory tree. In spite of my sporadic efforts to transfer fallen leaves to a compost pile I built in a particularly shady part of the garden, the ground is heavily blanketed with leaves.

I sometimes wonder about the squirrels that reside high above my back yard. When the weather is inclement and the wind roars, I think of their desperate condition in melodramatic terms, foreseeing death and destruction for them all. It is true that, after a blustery night, I find many small branches in the yard but no dead squirrels. These small animals must have made a pact with nature that, when they die, their bodies will disappear, mysteriously, soundlessly, without any of the clamorous grief that mars so many human burials.

When my older daughter was a preschooler, before she could even understand or realize the significance of the words she was saying, I taught her to recite some lines by the seventeenth-century English poet Robert Herrick. Brightly and, in my opinion, charmingly, she would walk about the house saying:

> When a daffodil I see,
> Hanging down his head toward me;
> Guess I may what I must be;
> First, I shall decline my head;
> Secondly, I shall be dead;
> Lastly, safely buried.

How better to conclude this essay on old age than with the innocent voice of my daughter speaking the sweet sounds of Herrick.

Paul F. Moran (1922–1995) spent his entire life working in libraries. From 1960 to 1985, he was in charge of the Bureau of Mines library. A lifetime non-smoker, he nevertheless developed lung cancer and, in retirement, fought a losing battle against it.

Oyasuteyama or the Mountain of the Old
Masako Saigo Cohen

A sad night was approaching for families who had old people living with them. In old villages in the northern part of Japan, custom called for the son in every household to take the old people somewhere far into the mountains and abandon them. These old people were their parents who had worked hard for the families. But it was necessary to make the old people die in the mountains because the villagers earned a precarious living and always lacked enough food for their families. This tragic event would take place on the fifteenth night of the eighth moon, the great full-moon night of the year. So the old people had to be gracefully resigned to their fate.

An old woman who had reached the age of abandonment finished her work for the family and divided her belongings among them before leaving. On that evening, moonlight flooded the sky. During their humble dinner, each family member gave her a sad farewell without saying a single word. By this time, the old woman's small body had been bent almost in two from old age. Her son said, "Mother, I'll take you there." She nodded to him with a smile, as if she were eager to go. The son put his mother on his back and headed for the high mountain behind the village. The mountain trail was so quiet that they could hear the singing of insects. When he was sure that she could never come back by herself, he put her down under a tree and fled. She knew her death was necessary for the well-being of the family, and so she would never shout after him vainly.

As he followed the trail back to the village, the son's eyes were filled with tears. When he laid himself down at the foot of the mountain, he could not sleep. This sad custom went on for a long time in the village. As for the mountain, it was known as the "Cursed Mountain for the Old."

Masako Cohen remembers hearing this story told during her childhood in Japan. See the biographical note on her after "The Jizos Wore Sedge Hats" (page 46).

Growth & Change

Who Says an Older Woman Can't/Shouldn't Dance?

Gloria Wade-Gayles

When you are fifty and over, people seem to feel the need to tell you how well you are physically wearing/weathering your age. Their evaluations are compliments, or perhaps I should say "condiments"–thick catsup, sweet jellies, creamy sauces, and brown gravy needed for meals we did not order and do not relish. In other words, they are intended to make palatable the unappetizing reality of growing older. "Don't let this go to your head," they caution, "but you really look good for your age." The compliments, so unoriginal, so tired, so cliché-ish, so focused exclusively on the physical, are, I suppose, the answers women want to hear when they ask, "Mirror, mirror on the wall, who's the best preserved of them all?" Those who hold the mirror for me have no idea that I am turning away in irritation. I mean, who gave them the right to assume that I need to be reassured about the good fight I am waging against the scarring hand of time? They compliment, and I talk back to them with my inside voice:

"How do you do it? You just don't look your age."
[Do what? Look how?]
"You're so playful so … so much fun. You don't act your age."
[I came out of my mother's womb playful, and pray tell me why I can't remain so at my age, and says who?]
"No gray hair? Come on now. I know you are using a rinse."
[Are you asking me or telling me?]
"It's the natural! That's the magic. People do say a natural takes years off a black woman's face. When I see how young it makes you look, I seriously consider giving up my perm."

[Give up your perm! You wouldn't go natural if guidelines for the crowning of Miss America required that the tiara be placed only on top of peppercorn.]

"You're the kind of older woman who could drive a young man crazy."

[That's supposed to be a compliment? All he needs to be is young, but I have to be some kind of special-old! Exactly what bait am I using to get this so-called catch?]

"It's amazing. You still look sexy."

[You need a crash course in sexuality after fifty.]

"Me. Personally, I prefer older women, unless they're fat. Now that, even in a young woman, turns me off."

[When was the last time you stepped on the scale, I wonder.]

"Girl, you're lucky. You don't have to worry about lying on top."

[Lying on top? What in the world is *that* about?]

"You know. When we lean over our sag really sags."

Age is a national obsession. Correction: *Aging.* That is the politically correct word for the addition of years to our lives, but I find it a sterile word, and therefore appropriate, I suppose, for the kind of reality women are supposed to have as we become older. It is flat like our breasts which (without implants) sag, cold like our feet, which we must cover with socks or risk "turning off" the man with whom we sleep, and colorless like the lives we are supposed to live. It lacks poetry, color, and movement. It is a neutering word that places us in clinical categories: premenopausal, menopausal, postmenopausal, losing this and needing that. Like a cold stethoscope pressed against our bosom, *"aging"* listens for a weaker heartbeat; or like an unfeeling gloved hand, it enters those parts of ourselves where we are most vulnerable. How much like "ailing" it sounds. Was *aging* always the naming word? I wonder. What was the word for my mother's generation and her mother's? Has anyone conducted research on the different words for this "affliction" and examined them in a political context? Always, there is a political context.

Age-and-gender biases are invisible particles in the air we breathe; they get into our bloodstream and change the chemistry of our attitudes toward other people and, if we are women, toward ourselves. In the media, they are the stark and seductive images that turn on the projector, amplify the sound, color the scenes, and write scripts that give leading lines to women who are young and only a nod to women who are older. To men, however, they give the enviable ability to be more attractive, more sexy, more suave, more everything desired precisely because they are older, even if age walks in deep crevices on their face. Like aged wine, older men, mellowed and smooth, become a desired vintage. Older women, on the other hand, are the tasteless wine, rendered flat from having been open so many years. Proof is the saying that older men are sexy, so much so that young women sometimes choose older men–graying temples and all–for their sex fantasies. There is no such saying for older women, and if they, by chance, enter the fantasies of younger men, we charge, "Oedipal!"

~

Nor are there Streep versions of older black women. Down through the centuries, we have been the "darker berry" (an *object!*) that gives "sweeter" juice, and recently we have become "freaks, superfreaks" no man would dare "take home to Mama." The "berry" and the "freak," like the pumping-grinding brother, are young. When we become older, we are neither berries nor freaks. We are, instead, neutered uncles and mammies. Bandannas, not ribbons, and aprons of asexuality, not dresses that catch the wind, are our media costumes. And how appropriate this is for a nation that created the asexual mammy in order to conceal the very sexual requirements of her role in the big house.

To be black, woman, and older is to be plunged whole into toxic waters from head to torso to heel, and we must find creative ways to prevent the damage from being consummate, for this triple jeopardy removes us from what this culture values: being white, being male, and being young. This is the case in the white world outside our communities, and no less so within our communities, for we have yet to develop immunities to the ailments white America suffers. We love young as much as we love white and we continue to privilege male over female.

Of course, we put the problem squarely on the shoulders of "the man." Before we were assimilated into white America, we say, or before we were Europeanized, we say, we valued the wisdom and beauty of older women. Like syphilis, we say, obsession with age is a disease we contracted from "them." My over-fifty way of thinking tells me that knowing who gave us the disease (as if we actually contracted it from "them" in particular rather than from human beings in general) does not remove it from our bloodstream. Once we have it, the search for a cure cannot take us away from ourselves. And a cure we *do* need. Older black women are the butt of offensive jokes in the black community. "Ain't nothing an *old* black woman can do for me" is a common punch line in comic routines, as is "Ain't nothing a *real* black woman can do for me" ("real" meaning very or "too").

I think becoming fifty made a "new woman" out of me. Shock treatment. That's what it was. I saw "Five O," I heard "half a century"; and I became determined to fight the demons that frighten us about age. My retina worked better than it ever had and my ear canal became long enough to be written up in the *Guinness Book of Records*. I began to see and to hear age biases I missed in my younger years. Sometimes I wish I didn't have this worrisome thing called awareness because it critiques the very pleasure out of a movie and jangles the chord of a song. It was that way with my awareness of misogyny ("Can't you just see the movie," my children used to ask, "and forget what's gender-wrong with it?"); and it has always been that way with my awareness of racism ("Don't you think you are being racially hypersensitive?" white friends ask). Sometimes when I am weary of the weight of awareness, I tell myself, "Just forget the lyrics, girl, and go on and dance to the beat." That is what I said when I recently bought a discounted CD containing the best hits by Ray Charles. I danced, as I had many years ago, to "Smack Dab in the Middle," a favorite of mine because it is Charles at his gospel-funk best, accompanied by his talking piano rather than symphonic strings which can't talk the way only Charles can. I danced, trying to ignore that the song objectifies women, putting us in a list of things Charles desires. I danced, trying to ignore a message I was hearing for he first time: that the women are desired only if they are young. Charles sings that he wants:

> *Ten Cadillacs.*
> *A diamond mill.*
> *Ten suits of clothes*
> *To dress to kill.*

Fierce with Reality

A ten-room house.
Some barbecue.
And twenty chicks
Not over twenty-two.

Am I jealous that I am not in the middle with the Cadillacs, the suits of clothes, the house, and the barbecue? Naw! I don't take well to being an object.

⌐

Unfortunately, all of the experts are white women. I wonder why we are not writing books about us and the addition of years? As with everything else, in this, too, we are unique. We can complain that we are not in *Passages*, *The Fountain of Age*, *Salty Old Women*, and *The Beauty Myth* (which is, in its own way, about age since beauty requires youth), but we don't have a varicosed leg to stand on if we do. The way that racism exacerbates ageism, which is further exacerbated by class, is our project and nobody else's. To paraphrase Langston Hughes, somebody oughta write a book about black women coping with the addition of years, and I guess it oughta be us.

Should I care that as a black woman in her fifties, I am consigned emotionally to one of three groups? Women who are depressed, made so by loneliness, regrets, and fear of a speedy decline into emptiness. Woman who are angry, made so by remembering too well who did them wrong, including themselves in the group. Women who are saintly, though I can't for the life of me understand what made this group, except perhaps the prescription that we begin preparing early for the afterlife to ensure that we walk on streets of gold rather than burn in furnaces. Saintly. Translation: bland and blind. We see no evil, speak no evil, do no evil, and for that matter, remember no past evil see, spoken, or done. By us, that is. Saintly? Translation: asexual.

Perhaps I dance because many of our mothers could not, or did not. Perhaps I dance because I am celebrating the liberation they did not experience, but wanted so desperately for their daughters. Perhaps I dance because their struggles and their sacrifices have blessed me with good-life rhythms they never heard. Perhaps I dance as a way of screaming against the dirges poor black women hear every day of their lives. Dirges are for death, not life. I want to live. I want to live as fully at fifty-plus, at sixty, and at seventy as I lived at twenty, thirty, and forty. I want to live and therefore I must dance. I dance, then in spite of my age and because of my age.

The first half-century of my life was the "yes" season. I could not shape my lips to answer "no" to others' needs or remember how to say "yes" to my own. I was always interruptible, always accessible and available, always willing to get out of a document that bore my name and pull up, on my own computer no less, someone else's document. I was like a plant from which one takes cuttings. A piece for this one. A piece for that one. A piece for those over there and these over here. Although there were times when I could feel the blade, I did not regret the cuttings. They strengthened my roots.

But there is a time when a plant should be left still, when the number of cuttings should be reduced, when it should be left undisturbed in the light of its own nourishing suns. Now is that time for me, and I am content in accepting that only now could the me-time have arrived. I believe I entered this season when I was supposed to. What remains is for me to do what I believe I am supposed to do: pick up the pen, or turn on the computer, and attempt to write.

When friends tell me that I should have tried to write years ago, planting seeds of regret in the earth of my feelings, I add rather than subtract, and the result is a full life of memories and experiences that form words and images I was not supposed to know, until now.

As I sing a soon-sixty song, I hear the same chords of meaning I have sung all of my singing life. They instruct me in how to work at living an examined life and how to *choose joy*. But of course *joy*, because sadness has no rhythm to which wrinkled hands can clap and to which varicosed legs can dance. Dance. *DANCE!*

Gloria Wade-Gayles, a former Woodrow Wilson Fellow and a DuBois Scholar at Harvard, was awarded the Emory University Medal for outstanding scholarship and service. In addition to *Rooted Against the Wind: Personal Essays*, she has authored three books and edited four anthologies. A native of Memphis, she is currently Eminent Scholar's Chair in Independent Scholarship at Spelman College, where she directs an oral history project on older African American women of the South.

The Flame

He was
fragile
and trans-
parent
like the
time-dimmed
glass of
an old oil
lamp, but
his pride
was the wick's
bright burning.
I longed to
steady his
steps, to
guide his
faltering
fingers
but the flame was hot.

Helen Earle Simcox

Helen Earle Simcox is the wife of a semi-retired Presbyterian pastor. They live in Columbus Ohio. Simcox is the author-illustrator of four picture books published by Windswept House, Mt. Desert, Maine, and one picture book published by Augsburg-Fortress in Minneapolis. She also edited and illustrated a book of Afro-American poetry, *Dear Dark Faces* (Lotus Press, Detroit, 1980). Her poems have appeared in literary journals and periodicals.

Red Shoes at Sixty

She dons red shoes
and is small again,
going to her first party.
Too poor—
too practical
all these years for
anything but neutral
go-with-everything hues,
she hankered secretly
for the heartening
magic of red.
She's like a garden
staging a grand finale
before the curtain
of winter falls—
one last fling
one last flaunting of
brave color
before the snow.

Helen Earle Simcox

Just Keep Breathing

Anna Morgan

Census takers, Social Security worrywarts, and doctors are warning that the number of people over ninety is increasing, as if we were a threatening pest like the African killer bees. With a lot of luck, people my age survived diseases, surgery, accidents, wars, and depressions, and surprised themselves by reaching ninety. Politicians accuse us of cluttering up the landscape. For example, the former Colorado governor, a man in his fifties, criticized us for living too long. But politicians ignore the fact that, for those few of us who reach ninety, millions of others did not live long enough to spend the Social Security money collected from them in their working days.

When people ask me, "To what do you ascribe your longevity," I always want to reply, "Shoo-fly, don't bother me!" But I smile sweetly, as a great-grandmother should, and give the most truthful answer I can think of, a quote from a long-forgotten woman, "Breathing, my dear. I just keep breathing."

Why are people so curious about our age once we develop wrinkles? Consider, for example, a sunny day in 1983 when I was marching up Tremont Street to the federal building in Boston to protest Reagan's sneak attack on Grenada. A brash young reporter, falling in step with me, stuck a mike in my face and shouted above the din, *"How old are you?"* as though my age were in any way related to the military invasion or the demonstration. I shouted back, "How old are *you?*" He was speechless a moment. Then he shouted, "I'm thirty-two. How old are you?" Talk about a one-track mind. I shouted, "I'm eighty-eight. Wanna do something about it?" I glanced over my shoulder, expecting to see other endangered species, like the Canadian baby seals, the great grey whales of the North Atlantic, or alligators from the Everglades. They weren't there–already extinct, no doubt.

But we of the ninety-plus clan are actually far from extinction. Certainly we are stronger, more active and more able to protest than the old were when I was a girl. Eighty years ago, people were old at sixty-five. In those days, woman of sixty-five wore a small black bonnet perched on top of her tightly pulled back white hair. Long black crepe ties knotted under the chin anchored the bonnet. To avoid a chill, she wore the traditional black summer tippet around her neck, a deep, six-inch collar on a fifteen-inch-wide circular, lined black shawl. If her husband were still alive, he wore a shiny black suit. His black Derby hat was as hard and stiff as the construction hat of a steel welder on a skyscraper. The tired old man walked slowly because, in his vest pocket on the end of a heavy chain, he wore a watch as large as a turnip, which dragged on him like the anchor of the old frigate *Constitution* in Charlestown.

These days, if I quote myself more often than I quote professors from the five universities around Boston, the *New York Times*, or the Washington cab drivers so often quoted on TV, it is because I know I have "all my buttons" as we used to say in the days when we wore high button shoes.

Some people in their nineties are ill, but some of us are healthy and want to be active. I protest against those extremely kind and well-meaning relatives, cooing syrupy platitudes, who pat us on the head while they firmly push us out of the way. Why should I sit in a creaky old rocker to please them when I'd rather be in the kitchen making a big vegetable soup or an apple pie for relatives coming to visit me? I do not try to stay young; one cannot. I don't want to move to a retirement colony, where the ads promise I can waltz all day. I want to live out my life in a community with good neighbors and grow old naturally, wrinkled like a winter Baldwin apple left in the bottom of the barrel until April. I want "smiling" wrinkles I can be proud of.

I read in the Boston paper one day that a local university wanted senior citizens to volunteer for a scientific study of diet. "Why not?" I asked myself. "It's a civic duty." I was thoroughly examined by an efficient young nurse and later told I was too old for the study. The cut-off age was seventy-nine. The researchers didn't give a whoop what I had eaten for ninety-four years to survive as an active, healthy, sane and optimistic woman.

Fierce with Reality

In my eighties, after my husband died, I visited the pyramids of Yucatan and found them more difficult to descend than ascend. In the same decade, I went to the Soviet Union and later checked up on the success of Fidel Castro's revolution. The people were so much better off than they were at the time of my first visit, sixty-five years earlier, that I came away content. I also went to Puerto Rico in the midst of an exciting political campaign. With a clipboard in hand, I covered San Juan, Ponce, and several smaller cities for three weeks, asking voters if they favored independence from the United States, always a hot issue. That was the most interesting vacation I could have had.

My nineties have brought problems, however. I began to hear bells in my head, for example. At first I ignored them, but when I heard voices constantly chattering, I remembered with alarm Joan of Arc in 1429 and rushed to Massachusetts General Hospital. Medication and a hearing aid brought me back to the 1980s. Later, when my cat repeatedly entered my room with a halo of purple and golden fringe, I suspected the cat was okay, but I was–? An ophthalmologist called it "glaucoma" (for a fee of over a hundred dollars), a problem in my eyes and not on the cat's head. And then my daughter discovered in the saucer with my round red pills some round red buttons from my old plaid dress. Red buttons are not a diuretic.

Senior citizens, if alert, recognize creeping ailments, such as twinges in the joints, and they suffer from recurring bouts of the flu. Our medical problems can be expensive. My advice is always to go to a young doctor who will speed you through his assembly line so rapidly that he won't take the time to discover a new and even more expensive ailment. If you live far out in the country, you can take care of yourself with a ten or twelve-pound medical book and a herb catalogue.

It is possible for a person my age to have more than sixty great-great-grandchildren in all shapes, sizes, and colors. As these characters develop and live their own lives, we can be shocked and, in time, even amused to discover around the Christmas tree or the Hanukkah bush nudists, vegetarians, CIA agents, nuns, communists, Rock-'n-Roll artists, skinheads, and euthanasians. It is impossible to know personally, much less to like, all of one's extended family, so I don't even try. I enjoy visits from relatives except if they come to borrow money. My closest, well-meaning relatives can be bothersome. They are always kindly picking a thread off my shoulder, or scanning my color combinations, or re-buttoning the twenty-odd buttons going down the front of my winter coat, or rubbing imaginary dust from the toes of my shoes. I can only smile and say, "I was just testing to see if you'd notice." To myself, I say, "I'm ninety-four; what's your excuse?"

Some people over ninety have lived so long in this tough, drab, unreasonable, violent, dishonest, noisy and crazy world that they just want to take off their shoes and go back to bed. They spend hours looking through a kaleidoscope, or making a cat's cradle with string while listening to soap operas. They are escapists. I'm a realist. I'm still hoping to improve the world.

Anna Morgan (1885–1996), an activist who took part in many progressive struggles beginning in the 1930s, died in 1996 at the age of 101. On her 100th birthday, she was pictured in the Somerville, MA paper riding her exercise bicycle. She was featured on a CBS special about centenarians.

Seasoning

Ida VSW Red

The young dyke says: "You don't *look* sixty-one–I can't *believe* you have children older than me." I'm tempted to correct her grammar and then respond as I heard one vital old lesbian do: "Take another look–this is exactly what seventy (or sixty-one or eighty) looks like!" But I know I'm just one of many ways to look and be sixty-one. Because I feel naive and green, I resent the common notion that age and experience necessarily produce wisdom. I don't know how to be old, but I realize that many elements, aspects, and states of being always coexist in me.

I am a ripened, grey dandelion head floating down Cripple Creek, allowing myself to tumble over and over, bump into boundaries, release seeds, round Russian River bends, and flow gaily forward.

I am a child's big, red rubber ball bouncing through a field of daisies to a mountain cabin where I rest by the open fire and marvel at the floor-to-ceiling cases of books I've been writing in my sleep.

By day, I read the obituaries, looking for women, scanning their lives, wondering how mine stacks up, trying to take credit for my accomplishments, such as fine, grown children; a long association with amateur theater; a librarian and editor's career completed; unfailing interest in poetry, autobiography, reading, writing, and performance; a first year of retirement rich with travel, grandchildren, work with *Mothertongue Feminist Theater Collective* and *Gay and Lesbian Outreach to Elders*, and new and old lovers and friends.

I am an exuberant and curious pigtailed five-year old on a swinging bridge … awkward teenagers opening Pandora's box … a young wife posing as a matron in a navy silk sheath … harried part-time, temporary, para-professional worker … mother of two, Brownie Scout leader, Sunday-school teacher … re-entry grad student always reading, wondering … beginning teacher in love with literature, ideas, my students, their writing … an actor publicly revealing details observed, feelings hidden, personalities submerged … a poet screeching to a halt mid-commute to catch the flicker of a lightning-bug phrase … an antique porch rocker with many coats of paint and lap enough for my little ones … a dreamer's open palm stretched out to catch a subtle distinction, a valuable connection.

My work at the University of California Institute for Health and Aging made me painfully aware on a daily basis of the ageism, poverty, chronic illness, and lack of social support faced by old people, especially old women. Like others in the glass house of aging policy research, I maintain a high level of denial, yet my internalized ageism and personal doubts and fears about aging are near the surface. Will I be able to remain financially, emotionally and physically independent? If not, will support be available, and will I accept it with grace? Will I have the courage to handle chronic illness or physical decline, the loss of loved ones, rapid changes in the world around me? Will my daughters respect me, and will we stay close, share our lives? Will I see my ideas and ambitions come to maturity?

I am a well-worn Appalachian dulcimer reverberating the strum of blue-ridged mountains, blue-grass fields trimmed in Queen Anne's lace, fringed chicory, brown-eyed Susan, and tough, tangled bittersweet bursting open at first frost.

I am a flat, gelatinous, silent eleven-year old, a pasty-faced chameleon who can only sit and watch since desperately trying to do as others do is a miserable failure and insisting on drawing the paperdolls my own way prompts ridicule—sit and watch, won't play, won't compete, won't try, won't just won't—

a blank tablet to be drawn on with a sharp stick, images that disappear when the shiny grey page is disturbed.

I can't read the weekly pink arts section in the newspaper. I am plunged into feelings of desperation and defeat by accounts of the accomplishments of actors, directors, and authors. I have given family and economic independence priority over intellectual and artistic work. Now I feel too discouraged, too outdated, too scared of memory loss to attempt a serious actor/writer/scholar's life. Caustic streams of envy, comparison, self-recrimination, and bitterness surge up and drive me to the shut-down, depressed emptiness that masquerades as ordinary life. Even going to the movies, usually a saving grace in which my inner process smooths itself out, is becoming painful. None of these feelings of hurt and loss is enough to jumpstart me into action. Instead, I insist on ordinary life's being enough. I latch onto it with a will, truly believing I deserve to have easy days in which to relax, drop my self-consciousness, and recover from a sense of having failed my family's expectations and my own.

I am a prickly animal, small, sensitive, low to the ground, hardly a threat until I unexpectedly shoot my piercing quills into some convenient, unsuspecting target.

I am a sea anemone, habitually clinging to my traditional place at great cost until I become too, too dry when I let go, float, give myself over to sea change.

I am a spider, flinging myself into the unknown, confident of finding a mooring for the web I create for myself, believing in survival, true to principle, faithful to community.

One of my first reactions to the early feminist idea of a woman-identified life was that, at forty, I was too old. I had never been independent. That was for modern young women like the first dyke I loved—fifteen years my junior, beginning her adult life in blue jeans. I had a hard time imagining a change of "lifestyle"—a new concept—at my age. While I was on a fence of indecision, a lesbian twelve years my senior forced me to notice her. She was both romantic and cynical, hidden and blatant, tough and soft. An evening in the presence of her vitality and a night caressing her beautifully aged skin convinced me that, for lesbians, there is no such thing as "too old." So I took the leap into dykedom. Now I am older than she was at that time. I haven't found the structures for equal relationships, lesbian theaters, and feminist doctoral programs I long for, but I nevertheless imagine that life is full of possibility at every turn.

I am a huge brown pre-pubescent bear poet named BoBo from Blue Rock Junction, lover of life, playful and serious, tender and fierce, self-published because typesetters could never get the rhythm of the Rs in my GRRs.

I am a galax leaf—large heart with sharp, ragged edges, ever-green, running wild, migrating toward the sunset.

I am a swashbuckler in chartreuse and fuchsia satin with cardboard boots, fake as the drugstore cowboy, authentic as my first family of Virginia genealogy with our mythical Spanish Gypsy, French sea explorer, and Native American among the predominantly German and English/Scotch/Irish farmers and merchants.

I am a heavy, inherited matriarchal mantle ... keepsakes cherished ... stories embroidered, braided, patchworked by generations of women: the common woman's fate—AND—love doves on a rainbow dragon kite ... interlocking women's symbol ... lesbian feminism: the seasoning ... a trail discovered from eastern virgin hemlock to Pacific shores.

I am a calliope with romantic ballads and old-fashioned roses magically transforming into a computer—both, descendants of a woman's weaving card—binary logic bent to aesthetic need and practical desire.

At my birthday party, when I told a friend's five-year old my age, she responded enthusiastically: "Wow! You'll *really* be a big girl now!" Age, size, and power seem wonderfully linked in her reality. On optimistic days, I agree, believing I will be able to continue living with lesbians who give our attention, courage, support, love, and inspiration to one another and help each other become our fullest selves, our strongest force for change.

> *I am a bearded crone simultaneously juggling zits and hot flashes for years on end … a color never seen … a biscuit baked with buttermilk and tears.*

> *I am a pile of slimy green overcooked spinach on the floor, crying, whining, complaining, pouting, too sad, too mad, too caught in misery some days to notice that …*

I am an aging woman, at sixty-one innocent and experienced enough to know my ball bounces on, fertile seeds constantly rise to celebrate existence, unknown paths await, new selves rush to join old ones in the miracle and mystery of the present moment.

I am &

Ida VSW Red is a 73-year-old lesbian feminist writer, actor, and group facilitator in the San Francisco Bay Area. Hailing from the Blue Ridge Mountains of Virginia and retired from the Institute for Health & Aging, University of California, Red wrote and performed with Mothertongue Feminist Theater Collective for twenty years and has been published in several lesbian anthologies and journals.

Being Old

Nina Draxten

In 1864, when he was fifty-two, Robert Browning wrote a poem beginning:

> Grow old along with me!
> The best is yet to be,
> The last of life for which the first was made.

At times I have thought the poet did not know what he was talking about when he wrote, "Rabbi Ben Ezra," from which this quotation is taken. Now that I have grown old myself, I see that the poem is an affirmation of the on-going value of life.

Old people have the same needs as everyone else: good health, including the ability to move about freely; the companionship of persons of various ages, not limited to other old people; and a daily life that carries with it some element of surprise. The first is the most important; the other two can be maneuvered into one's life. I can explain this best by recounting my life as an octogenarian.

At eighty-six, I am lucky, for I am healthy and can move about freely. In spite of Minnesota's arctic winters, I went about with an uncovered head, a light-weight jacket, and low-cut shoes, usually, rather than overshoes or boots. People warned me that I would one day be crippled with arthritis or rheumatism, but, other than a slight ache in a joint, which disappears after a brief massage, I have no trouble. I smoked for forty years, an average of a pack a day, until the Surgeon General warned of the health hazard from smoking. I endured the agony of withdrawal and have been tobacco free for more than thirty years.

I worked as a teacher, beginning with high school in Wisconsin and eventually moving up to college teaching. I enjoyed teaching but not writing articles on educational subjects. In my sixties, I came upon some material about Kristofer Janson, a poet and novelist who was a friend of Henrik Ibsen and Bjornstierne Bjornson and who had lived in Minneapolis for twelve years. The story of Kristofer and his wife, Trude, was so fascinating that I wondered why no one had made use of the material before. I embarked on a biography of the man, limited to his life in America. That meant primary research, combing through Norwegian language and sometimes Danish weeklies of the 1880s and early 1890s, besides the material in English, which also proved to be abundant. I published articles from these sources. At that time, the University of Minnesota, where I taught, permitted faculty members to teach until they were sixty-eight, but I felt that I would never finish my book unless I could devote full time to it. Therefore, I retired at sixty-five and published the book in 1976, when I was seventy-three. It was widely and favorably reviewed in the scholarly journals.

At the time, my brother and I were living in our childhood home where we had a common circle of friends. He was younger than I, and, when he retired in 1976, we belonged to the same study club and had season tickets to concerts. I began a second book again working in archives. In mid-1984, I was busy writing when my brother died very suddenly. It was the most devastating blow I ever had; it was impossible for me to continue writing. My eighty-first birthday was two months away.

I had never lived alone before. For years my brother had done all the driving, and I didn't know where my license might be. I knew nothing about our furnace or details about the upkeep of a house. At times I tried to return to writing, but, no matter where I looked, I was reminded of my loss and absorbed in my sorrow.

I kept wishing I had some work that, for an interval at least, would take my mind off my bereavement. Finally, it occurred to me that I could do television commercials. In the 1920s, I had given some impersonations–a form of entertainment then popular–and during my years as a high school and college teacher had directed plays. I was afraid to call an agency, however, dreading a brush-off. One day on a city bus, I got into a conversation with a TV performer because of an incident we had both witnessed on the bus. Somehow I told her of my misgivings about calling an agency, and she encouraged me to call several.

Finally, I called the most prominent agency in Minneapolis. I asked to speak to someone about working in television. My first words were,

"I'm eighty-one years old." The woman at the agency asked, "And you can still get around?"

I was asked to bring pictures to the office. Fortunately, I had many pictures from a recent visit to my nephew's. I was cordially received at the office. After filling out cards on my dress size, shoe size, and the color of my hair and eyes, I was asked to read a blurb about a fictitious Johnson's soup and then was told that I would be called for auditions when the agency received a call for a person of my type. Shortly afterward, Burger King began auditions for the Herb commercials, a series that ran for several months. The filming took place in New York.

As other jobs followed, I was introduced into a totally new world of actors and actresses and young people aspiring to enter the profession. I found the latter very interesting. Often they did not make enough money to support themselves acting and had to depend on jobs such as waiting tables or painting houses. A comraderie existed among aspirants for jobs in spite of their rivalry.

After doing a number of television commercials, I was asked to audition for a motion picture written and directed by Sam Shepard. Luckily I was chosen and had the good fortune to work with accomplished actors such as Jessica Lange, Charles Durning, Tess Harper, and others, all of whom were gracious to an old lady who, so to speak, came in out of the cold. When the picture, *Far North*, was shown, I received quite a bit of attention as one who had become a motion picture actress at eighty-three. Early in 1989, when I appeared on the Pat Sajak show, a clip from *Far North* was shown.

Eventually, I was able to get back to my writing, and I published my second biography in 1988. Through my writing and my work as an actress, I have made many friends. Consequently, I have had a richer social life than would have been available to me as an inactive octogenarian.

Soon I will visit Norway. I was there once, sixty years ago, and, as I have changed in the interim, I am sure Norway has changed as well. This time, my way will be paid. I have the opportunity to go because I am healthy and can move about freely.

Nina Draxten (1904-2002), a retired English professor at the University of Minnesota and later an actor, died at the age of 98. She wrote two biographies, one of a Lutheran minister in Minneapolis and the other about a Norwegian who organized Unitarian churches in the Midwest in the 1880s.

Elsa: I Come with My Songs

excerpt from Elsa Gidlow's autobiography

Introduction by Celeste West

Elsa and I were heart-friends for fifteen years. She was a wise and vivacious poet in her seventies when we met, I in my twenties. From England by way of Montreal and New York City, Elsa overcame deep poverty and tragedy to create Druid Heights, a magnificent homestead in the northern California redwoods. It became known to many women as something of a lesbian Avalon. She made me feel special, interesting, and she shared her wise and acerbic insights with genuine passion. She was especially energized by the powerful wave of feminism both validating her and enlivening her as a life-long lover of feminine energy.

Elsa became a muse of *savior faire* and *savior vivre* to me. She profoundly delighted in all the ways the earth's and women's sensual natures manifest spirituality. At the same time, she ran a tight ship, too stern for some. Elsa could be as frugal and routine-conscious as a Zen priest high on discipline. I came to realize how small routines and rituals provide safe passage as one's world becomes more fragile with age.

When Elsa was eighty-four, we deepened our friendship by working together. I coordinated the publication of her collection of erotic poetry, *Sapphic Songs*, then her autobiography. Along the way, I filled notebooks with her "lessons," although she believed we teach one another and despised the male guru/student power dynamic. "Be careful," a woman said to me, "like Zen, she may break your heart." She did, of course, and then caused it to open again and again. When she was harsh and demanding, I got through by asking myself some of her favorite questions, "Is what seems to be happening the *real* story, or only a part, or an intermission to get us through?" "Perhaps this is a test?" Elsa's own tests were far greater than mine. "Luckily, I'm older and wiser," she said.

I broke down crying once, admitting that I was afraid she would die. "Nonsense," she said, "today I am an old woman, not a dead one." We decided to accept the very word "deadline" with jovial good sense, to simply end the autobiography if need be with the six words from a sign I met while hiking at Druid Heights, "Road Closed to Return to Nature." Nature turned out to be patient. The autobiography came out in the spring of 1986, and Elsa was ecstatic. She died that summer.

As Elsa opened her own heart again and again to her challenges, I saw how sheer doggedness, humor, and love in the present can light a very uncertain future. Finally bed-ridden, Elsa took about a month to let go. She simply stopped eating. There was pain, occasional resistance to physical systems going down, but her death was so much easier than others I had seen. Except for her precious cat, it was we in her "circle of care" who were befuddled and suffering. She told us to flip a coin regarding esoteric Buddhist burial questions. Elsa seemed to be silently gathering force, calmly contemplating her essence just as she always had in order to transform things. As she journeyed beyond words, I felt that no matter how hard it was, she knew exactly what she was going, midwifing something, "growing" as May Sarton put it, "toward the light."

Elsa's winter solstice fire ritual is a ritual of remembering, touching souls with our foremothers, then, with their help, focusing our own deep transformative powers, symbolized in the ritual of fire. It began at a time when she had lost everything: her great love of thirteen years had died of cancer; a tentative new relationship was over; books accepted for publication were killed due to wartime paper shortages; and freelance journalism offered no financial security.

With her last $700 she bought "a huddle of wood that no one else would consider a house." Alone during the Yule season, Elsa was terrified by the torrential rains that lashed the cabin. Would the fireplace draw to provide any warmth or light? The fire not only started, it roared into triumphant retort to the storm.

She thought she was alone. "Yet, as I added twigs and dry boughs, then madrone logs, the firelit room became peopled by presences: spirits of women. Women I had known: mother, grandmother, elder aunts, and back, back, all the women through the ages who kindled and tended sacred and domestic fires." Elsa describes a profound mystical vision, all her "mothers" connecting her to the Great Mother beyond isolation and loneliness.

She saved a charcoal log left after this Solstice fire and wrapped it in foil tied with a piece of red ribbon. It became the first of all her Solstice Yule logs, each one to rekindle the next. Her great poem "Chains of Fires," much anthologized, was shaped from this ritual.

Several of us now have "seeds" of Elsa's last Yule log. Here is one form of Elsa's evolving ritual we do on the longest night of the year. We first bless the seed of charcoal, the wood nourished by earth, air, and water, its blackness storing the birth of the sun. The room is dark, the longest night of the year. As the flames rise, each woman, one by one, approaches the fire, "trances" into it, and offers a small pine bough. The needles flare up as each woman silently names something from the year she wants to let go. She bows and pauses to say good-bye. Then she lights a new candle from the fire. At the end of the ritual, the room is a festival of lights. We all lift our candles in a shout to the "Awakening of the Light." Each woman takes her candle home to light her next year's Solstice fire and other "chains of fire" with loved ones.

from Elsa: I Come with My Songs

It's just over the edge of the Autumn Equinox. Here at Druid Heights, it is still dawn. The southeast sky begins to take on color like the watery inside of an abalone shell. Diamondy glints from the uppermost lance-like leaves of the towering eucalyptus trees beyond the garden announce the rising sun, although at ground level we are still in the twilight of receding night.

These moments, this hour, between dark and light, between sleep and waking, between our deepest inwardness and the push-pull of an expectant world, are for me the most renewing of the diurnal cycle. This dawn, facing the year's decline as we begin to move through the Winter Solstice–feeling it more imminent since the recent blessing of early rain– there is the additional awareness of being between life and death.

This dawn I am aware of it and that such awareness enhances my life. There is delight in each ordinary act. Last night I died into sleep, and this dawn I am alive for the gift of another day. I have laid the fire to accompany breakfast but not yet lighted it. A first cup of fragrant Chinese tea warms and wakes my insides. A quartered, cored apple from the thirty-year-old Gravenstein that has been so generous this year waits on the tray with hot oatmeal porridge. But before these and an hour's meditation, or reading or writing, there are a few tasks with which I greet and become reacquainted with what is immediately outside.

The emerging seedlings of salad greens and winter vegetables must be watered before the sun climbs. I am grateful to see the just-transplanted bib, oak-leaf, and romaine lettuces sitting up fresh and thriving. The snow-pea vines, which like the mild, moist weather, are beginning to grasp the chicken wire support with their hairlike tendrils. The bok choy is several inches high and ready for thinning, as is the Chinese cabbage. I welcome the first green tips of the rutabagas, whose hearty roots should be swelling as the sun strengthens after the winter Solstice. The exuberant growth of the roquette, which faithfully seeds itself, is already enhancing my salad. I greet them all in grateful acknowledgment of their promise of nourishment and health as I gently spray them.

I see a doe with two fawns grazing through the fence, attracted perhaps by the sound or smell of water. There is not much that is succulent for them now. I take a pailful of fallen and bird-damaged apples and place it for them some distance from the garden. On my way back, I pick up an armful of sticks and eucalyptus bark to kindle tomorrow morning's fire.

The lighting of that dawn fire will lead me to the Winter Solstice Fire of annual renewal and link me to women throughout the ages–to their first capturing and domesticating of the sacred flame. This morning I feel those linkages most strongly as I sense the year's decline. *Decline.* I reflect on the word, the concept. What does it mean–in its deepest sense? What does it mean to me who will soon cross the calendar line to my eighty-seventh year?

Looking outward to the autumn world, I perceived ripeness, dissolution, decay into what is called death. But where the stalks and leaves have rotted, they have been transformed into compost, loam, to a seething workshop, a laboratory of elements and organisms that are feeding the peas, lettuces, root vegetables, herbs–what can be said of this death? What can be said of my death in this year's "decline" as I look to another birthday? Probing deeply, I try to realize, make real–death, my death–and can find no sense of it. What I do feel is the compost of my increasing years' amalgam of work, writing, love, joys, pain, hopes and disillusionments, defeats and triumphs. Many of these, as they performed their alternating or interacting dance, come disguised as their opposites. So, too, I envision Life/Death inextricably bound together in an unceasing dance where each assumes the mask of the other, surrenders to the other, in perpetual metamorphoses.

Yes—I hear you: as a functioning, physical being, I have less capability where strength and endurance are required. Emotionally, I become more detached. The passions, if there is occasion for them, are less ardent, infrequently felt. But everything to its season. Is there not compensation in increased intensity of awareness? In the clear light of spirit shining out through ordinary phenomena? In the greater perspective on the significance and connection of events, personal and on the larger scene?

I ask: if there is a reservoir of creative consciousness on which all emerging life—not solely the human–draws, and each returns to that reservoir the fruits of its life experiences, what have I been contributing in exchange for my debt, what shall I render back when breath is surrendered? The physical elements composing the visible "me" face their obvious dissolution to reusable material. What, in the cauldron of my soul has been invisibly alchemized for rendering back? I do not know. I am willing to abide by the mystery and to celebrate it. This I shall do as I die into each night's sleep that is rehearsal for the final one, just as each dawn's awakening is rehearsal for–what?

Celeste West's works as a booklegger include *Lesbian Love Advisor, Words in Our Pockets*, and *Revolting Librarians*. Celeste also manages the library/bookstore at the San Francisco Zen Center.

Elsa Gidlow (1898-1986), an irrepressible free thinker and free heart, wrote the first American North American poetry book to celebrate love between women, *On a Grey Thread* (1923). Very prolific, Gidlow triumphed over poverty, lack of formal education, and family tragedy to found "Druid Heights," a Taoist inspired retreat among the California redwoods. Gidlow is featured in the film *Word is Out*.

Memory Is as Uncertain as Grace

Mary Meigs

1983: Four of us gather, all lesbians just below or just above senior status, two who have been married and divorced and have grown children, and two who have never married. Our purpose is to discuss aging. I have sought out the others to enlarge or confirm my own experience and find that we have much in common, particularly a determination to make the changes of age work for us, to make new creative constellations of changes that are forced on us. All four of us are still actively thinking and working. Jane Gapen, Barbara Deming, and I are painters or writers or both who have always had a sense of vocation. Ruth, who has changed her married surname to Dreamdigger, did not feel herself to be an artist and did not suffer the frustration, as Jane did, of an artist-mother. Her children are a source of deep happiness to her. Her vocation has been non-violent action for peace and against nuclear weapons and the study of human relations; she has worked with disturbed and economically deprived children and, though nominally retired, now belongs to the Movement for a New Society, an organization stressing personal growth. She works in conflict resolution and peer counseling. She was moved to change her name to Dreamdigger because she uses dreams to understand herself and, in her work with others, not to discover neuroses as Freud did, but to discover the multiple layers of conscious and unconscious being, the creative complexity of every human being. Jane Gapen, who has written a fictional autobiography, *Something Not Yet Ended,* is also a poet and a painter and is now concentrating on painting. She says that, as an aging woman, she can more fully express her creative life in painting than in words. As I look at her recent work, I feel that the poet and the painter are still in equilibrium and that she has found a visual poetic language for states of being beyond words. But, at this point in the conversation, when Jane is suggesting that *looking* inward and outward is more in harmony with the physical truth of her aging, I say that I now have the impulse both to look and to push and prod my brain and force it to think. "Writing is what makes me know my mind is alive," I say. Later, writing this, I feel this aliveness, sitting on a platform built on the spreading branches of a big banyan tree, leaning against one of its thick trunks, as I think about our four-way conversation and watch two warblers hop along the branches above me and a turkey vulture sail overhead close enough to see its red hood, and it seems to me that the integration of thinking and seeing and finding both words and images is as essential to me as the circulation of my blood.

We all agree about two things: that we have less energy than we used to and that we do things more slowly. We like to do things at our own pace, and we hate to be hurried. We take longer to get started in the morning; we putter around; we forget what we are looking for in the refrigerator; we forget names. Forgetfulness and how to combat it is something we discuss with eager despair. We all make lists. I say I like to make lists of things to be done, then to check them off one by one. Jane says that the making of a list tempts her to think that the things *have* to be done. But lists do not prevent us from having the blanks that seem to accompany the effort to remember something. These blanks are like an impenetrable fog imposed between the mind and what it seeks to remember. A certain amount of forcing will further thought, but memory is as uncertain as grace; no effort will summon it, only the paradox of forgetting what one wants to remember. Then the memory will suddenly appear, perhaps the next day, like a tropical fish swimming in front of one's mind. The patience to wait to remember has to be learned. Barbara thinks of these thought-blanks as times of unconscious growth; she loses herself in them and finds that, just as sleep solves problems, so blanks have their subconscious power to clarify thought that will only get muddled if it is forced. Age gives us leisure to turn what may seem like its negative aspects—absent-mindedness, forgetfulness—into states akin to trance. Barbara has always complained about her slow and painful struggle to think and write, but her work is evidence of the creative energy of meditation, and aging provides new forms of meditation.

Both Barbara and Jane seem to float with the current of age, almost to welcome the reasons it gives them to live in harmony with the physical process of aging. Ruth uses memory to coax dreams up from the subconscious, and her creative life consists of digging out the multiplicity of meaning in her own dreams and those of others and using them as a path to understanding. Every day's harvest of dreams expands her cosmos of images and of clues to human behavior. It is an endless source of nourishment, unaffected by age. I say that my forgetfulness has begun to prevent me from remembering dreams, that those I remember are fragments that have none of the old beauty and resonances. But she insists that I can train myself to remember.

When we talk about physical symptoms apart from forgetfulness, we all laugh. My hands don't obey me as well, I say. I drop things. Barbara says that her hands tremble so that she can no longer do speed writing, or rather that she can't read what she has written and has to give up, a real grief to her. And one realizes, reading her work, how important speed writing has been to her when she wanted to write accounts of conversations or meetings as immediate and true as life. Nor can she type as fast and surely as she used to. And I think of my own fear—that my own hands, which have begun to draw quivering lines on occasion, will refuse my instructions to make a detailed drawing or to control the painting of the eyes or the mouth in a portrait. I remember hearing that Renoir, with a paintbrush strapped to his arthritic right hand, was able, having looked intently at his portrait, to place a highlight precisely in an eye. If one has never tried to do this, one cannot know the difference a fraction of an inch can make in the direction the eye is looking or its intensity. Renoir was guided by a lifetime of accuracy like a Zen archer; perhaps my shakiness will move me in the direction of greater freedom and less fussiness. Our disabilities have to be turned to use in the sense of opening new ways.

Still, there are disabilities that cannot be transformed, that take the form of annoyances and restrictions. All four of us get tired easily and have to go to bed relatively early. I fall into what I call my stupors, days when nothing seems to work, body or mind, when the mind is like a leftover pudding, and the body feels infinitely old and creaky. We laugh over our nights, punctuated by trips to the bathroom, by the fear sometimes of not getting there quickly enough, by having to get back to sleep again—

as though we were waked by an alarm clock two or three times a night.

We all agree about the life-giving aspect of having come out as lesbians. I have found my life as a writer. I have shed my fears and am no longer selective and defensive with my siblings. I have many new friends and a new sense of ease with them. All this happened after the age of fifty-five and is still true ten years later. I have never found that age makes me invisible to other lesbians even when I am the only senior lesbian present in a group, as I often am in Quebec. There is more emphasis on looking young among lesbians in Quebec than there is in the United States. I know senior lesbians who dye their hair, have their faces lifted, and have the satisfaction of feeling younger when they do these things. I do not think that every effort to resist the visible effects of aging should be blamed on the patriarchy; it can be a way of saying, "I look younger to myself; therefore, I feel younger." I, too, feel younger when I am sunburnt, when the brown spots of old age on my hands seem to vanish.

As I think about aging, I realize that I have not yet begun to suffer from the general contempt for older women and from a sense of my invisibility. I have only felt it once, last year in Italy when I saw myself as I was seen there—a white-haired old woman wearing slacks and running shoes, without a wedding ring, without a husband, when the stereotype of the old-maid lesbian was clamped on me inescapably and prompted a quite unfamiliar kind of rudeness and impatience. Some people, both men and women, went out of their way to be helpful, but, for the first time, it came to me as a shock what it means in a macho country to be old and single. And, too, for the first time, I felt literally invisible to the young. When I went to France, I encountered single women more or less like me, and, in Quebec, I was back in the land where lesbians, old or young, recognize each other and exchange smiles.

Quite recently, the problem of ageism has become a topic for discussion in feminist consciousness-raising sessions and, like many once invisible minorities, aging women are becoming vocal and visible. Remarkable books have been written in the last decade, such as May Sarton's novel, *As We Are Now*, in which the rest home where Caro, the aging heroine is confined, is a metaphor for the ugly psychological and physical suffocation that old age can bring. Like that other Caro in *The Stone Angel*, this one preserves a precious remnant of dignity and dies with it. Another book written by an aging woman is *Look Me in the Eye* by Barbara Macdonald and Cynthia Rich, her younger lover, in which they look unsparingly at the patriarchy's imposed view of old women and its blueprint for them.

We four who are talking are lucky to have each other and to be part of the wider conversation and sharing of experience of all women. In the course of our talk, I ask the two mothers what it has meant to them to be mothers, if it is comforting now as they enter old age. Jane says, "Well, motherhood is one of the sacraments." Another of the sacraments is art, she thinks; art, too, is giving birth, as necessary to the human spirit as biological birth. Jane has lived through difficult times with her children, but now they are there for her; they phone her, they worry about her, are friends. I ask her if her idea about the sacrament of motherhood doesn't give her a kind of absolution, a sense of having the right to be a lesbian because she has sacrificed to the patriarchal idea of women's role. I say that those of us who didn't want to be mothers have felt the obligation to work twice as hard to prove ourselves as artists, to overcome society's wish to diminish us, as women artists and as lesbians. Jane's life as an artist was slowed by years of child care, but the children seem to have enriched the very life that was slowed down by them. Ruth was able to combine her children with her outside work and says that they have always given her great joy. She describes Christmas in her old house in West Philadelphia, when her biological family together with her ex-husband and her "hodaka" family were gathered happily together. She has discovered the widest meaning of "family." She has lived the whole spectrum of women's experience: as lover (she had men lovers before her marriage), as wife and mother and grandmother and now as lesbian. She has a feeling of completeness, and her work with dreams and Tarot cards is completing her in a new way, in the unity of conscious and subconscious.

It is striking that none of us has a feeling of bitterness or defeat or of the horror of old age. I think this is true, for Jane and Barbara and me, at least, because the old woman artist, lesbian or not, is respected even by patriarchal society. She has survived, and she is allowed her physical disabilities and eccentricities if she produces acceptable evidence of herself as artist. One thinks of Georgia O'Keefe or Sonya Delaunay, or Kathe Kollwitz and Emily Carr. The older we get without falling into senility, the more we surprise people by the fact that we are still there, still working.

Lesbian artists over sixty-five who have come out are likely to be snubbed or obliterated by the patriarchy, but that, too, is changing little by little, partly because of those who have come out posthumously, so to speak, through disclosures about their lives: Willa Cather, Ivy Compton-Burnett, Elizabeth Bishop—all of whom have such a secure place in literature that they cannot now be excommunicated because they were lesbians. These women who kept their secret until they died give added power to aging lesbian artists and to aging women in general—the old-woman power which is essential to all of us, old and young, engaged in the feminist revolution.

Six years later: The community of lesbians at Sugarloaf Key lost its keystone with the death of Barbara Deming in the summer of 1984. I was there again in February 1989 and met with Ruth Dreamdigger and Jane Gapen to update our experience of aging. We still feel Barbara's absence, but her presence seems very strong. The breadfruit tree we gave her just before she died is putting out a new crown of green leaves. A black-crowned night heron she loved turns up as a familiar spirit (we have named her Barbara), sits on a roof and says, "Quawk." A couple of red-bellied woodpeckers are waiting impatiently for the papayas to ripen, and the huge fig tree is full of warblers and white-crowned pigeons. On the night of the full moon, we hold a moon ceremony, build a fire, and dance around the flowing embers at the center of the circle.

At our meeting, Ruth and Jane and I agree that we feel older than in 1983 (we are sixty-eight, sixty-nine and seventy-one now), but the effect of aging on each is different. Jane says she does things more slowly and that her mind bogs down in the middle of a sentence; she can no longer find the words to express what she means. But when I go to her studio, I see that she has done a lot of new work and is playing in a new way with color and space. What I said six years ago is still true: she has found a visual poetic language for states of being beyond words.

Ruth is engaged in new projects that keep her busy with the Unitarian Church in Key West as a new focus. She has less physical energy, but she is charged with a wonderful brightness and keenness of spirit. As always, she reads my Tarot cards and analyzes my dreams; as usual, the cards are full of clues to my present psychic state, and she gives me wise counsel.

In the past year, I've been lucky to witness the power of women my age. Seven of us were in semi-documentary film last summer (*The Bus,* made by th National Film Board of Canada) that turned out to be one of the happiest times of our lives. In the long spaces between film shots, we had time to exchange memories, to laugh endlessly, to sing and to dance. My next book will be about this experience of a magic place where each of us could speak out of the truth of her life. For six weeks, we were detached from patriarchal time and became indissolubly bonded as old women. We keep in touch with each other now, check up on each other's health, meet at parties (the last one was given by Constance Garneau, who had just turned eighty-nine. "I'm in my ninetieth year," she said proudly).

I can speak only for those of us who are not completely alone, living in poverty, or hospitalized with a crippling disease. The experience of *The Bus* led me to believe that old age can free women to live new lives, detached from the patriarchy. Even as a lesbian (I was the only lesbian in the film), I find that, as I grow older, the last remaining patriarchal shackles—guilts and self-imposed obligations–seem to fall off one by one and I've way to imperturbable defiance. [Jane Gapen died in 1992.]

Mary Meigs (1917–2002) was born in Philadelphia and lived in Montreal for many years. A painter, she had one-woman shows in Boston, New York, Paris, and Montreal. Her first book, *Lily Briscoe: a Self-Portrait*, was published in 1981. Meigs appeared in the film *Strangers in Good Company* and later published a book about the experience, *In the Company of Strangers*, 1991.

Mrs. Sheldon's Gift

Jane DiMillo

I picked up my large brown manila envelope from the debris littering the dining room table and checked its contents: ten index cards with neatly printed names and addresses, ten receipts slips, a small stubby pencil, a name tag saying "Hello, my name is …" I had offered to collect for this worthwhile cause, thinking it would be a reprieve from the grasps of little hands, the demands of dirty dishes waiting to be hoisted up and into the dishwasher, and the unspoken shame of unmade beds. But as I heard the sleet peck at the kitchen windows, I had second thoughts. However, tomorrow was the deadline.

I began my journey up the hill and across the street to the block of houses facing the elementary school. The first house was a disheveled piece of property. The driveway was car less, the kitchen windows naked except for the small darkening squares of evening slowly filling their panes. I turned into the driveway and climbed the back stairs.

Peeking through the back door's window into a narrow, dimly-lit kitchen, I spied the back of a figure sitting at the table. I knocked. The figure didn't move. I knocked again and this time the person heard me. She turned, saw me, and tried to rise from her chair. She tried again and was successful.

The woman peered out at me and adjusted her glasses. I raised my brown manila envelope and mouthed "American Heart Association." Her lips, like the locked door, remained closed.

"I don't have much money," she said, fumbling with the lock.

"Whatever you can give would be appreciated."

"Come in then, come in. You're letting the heat out."

She directed me to a nearby chair. The room was narrow: the kitchen table hugged the wall, allowing a thin passageway between the stove and refrigerator. "Don't mind the mess. Sit down." She swiped at the table in an attempt to clear a space. The room smelled of old newspapers and last night's pork chop.

Stacks of papers and magazines topped the chairs, the table, and the sideboard. She switched on the overhead light, but that didn't clear the view, just confused it. It appeared that her meals consisted of coffee-stained papers, stacks of magazine, fillets of notes, and rolls of broken pencils. I placed the chair-top contents down on the faded linoleum and hoped that the caned seat would hold me.

"Do you like to write?" she asked, fumbling through the contents in front of her. "I'm a writer, you know; but I can't seem to find anything these days." Baby barrettes prevented her fine, white hair from clouding her vision. Her wide mouth grimaced in frustration. She turned over slips of paper looking for her script of yesterday. "Look at this mess," she said, sifting the small rectangular pieces through her arthritic fingers. "I had an idea for a story, a good one."

"I like to write, but I don't have time." I said. "Little ones, you know."

She stopped rifling the contents in front of her and looked up at me. I wiped the sleet's moisture from my cheek. My confession embarrassed me. I had not admitted to anyone my passion for writing, a desire that I had flaunted as a child, bribing my friends with promises of pennies if they would just come and sit on my back porch while I acted out my little dramas, written hurriedly in the seclusion of a nearby shed. I had discarded those attempts as unimportant to anyone but me. So I pulled my chair closer to the table. "Journal sometimes." I said, discovering the salt shaker at the bottom of a pile. "Maybe when the kids get older."

"Don't wait," she warned. "Look at me."

I did look at her, a woman perhaps in her seventies, living alone, writing on scraps of paper, and intending to collect and organize them and develop them one day into stories. I promised her I wouldn't wait.

Mrs. Sheldon's fingers landed on a small leather purse. She tugged and pulled out two one-dollar bills. "Here, that's all I can afford."

I thanked her. She had given me more than enough. I began writing again in spurts generated by emotions or events and hid these manuscripts in the bottom of my desk; but often when passing Mrs. Sheldon's house, or waiting for the kids, I would remember my promise to take my writing seriously. Years later, after the children left for college and careers, I noticed a small article in the local paper about a writing program named Stonecoast. I still had the desire but lacked the funds. I worked and saved and took out loans. Then I applied and was accepted as a student in the Stonecoast Writers' MFA Program.

The night of my graduation as I viewed myself in the mirror, I saw a white-haired woman in her early sixties, filled with excitement, joy, and determination, and when I walked across the stage to receive my diploma, I heard the applause of the audience and felt the presence of Mrs. Sheldon. "Thank you," I whispered, "What a precious gift!"

Jane DiMillo teaches writing at the University of Southern Maine. She is currently working on a memoir titled *Veiled Moments,* a reflection on her years as a nun. Her published articles include "Telling Our Stories," "Philosophy of Adult Education," and "Spare the Rod."

Defiance & Self-Determination

The Last Words of My English Grandmother

There were some dirty plates
and a glass of milk
beside her on a small table
near the rank, disheveled bed—

Wrinkled and nearly blind
she lay and snored
rousing with anger in her tones
to cry for food,

Gimme something to eat—
They're starving me—
I'm all right I won't go
to the hospital. No, no, no

Give me something to eat
Let me take you
to the hospital, I said
and after you are well

you can do as you please.
She smiled, Yes
you do what you please first
then I can do what I please—

Oh, oh, oh! she cried
as the ambulance men lifted
her to the stretcher—
Is this what you call

making me comfortable?
By now her mind was clear—

Oh you think you're smart
you young people.

She said, but I'll tell you
you don't know anything.
Then we started
on the way

We passed a long row
of elms. She looked at them
awhile out of
the ambulance window and said,

What are all those
fuzzy-looking things out there?
Trees? Well, I'm tired
of them and rolled her head away.

William Carlos Williams

William Carlos Williams (1883–1963), poet and physician, lived most of his life in New Jersey. He was also a playwright and novelist. His plain speech and direct observation aligned him with the Imagist Movement in modern American poetry. He won the National Book Award for poetry in 1950 and the Pulitzer Prize in 1962.

Birthday Check

Aunt Lil sends me a card
folded around a check for $10
as she has done every year
since I gave her Mother's
red wool winter coat,
after the funeral.

She took it,
spoke of its warmth,
color, fit,
then added,
"Of course, you understand,
I can't take charity."

In her ninety-seventh spring
she writes the check
with a shaky pen,
seals the stamped envelope,
gives it to the mailman
on the right day
to reach me
on March 14th
as it has for twenty-two years
making this
the most expensive coat
Aunt Lil
has ever owned
in her
tightly budgeted life.

Marilyn J. Boe

"Birthday Check" first appeared in *Hurricane Alice*, vol. 5, No. 1 (1987).

A Mistaken Charity

Mary E. Wilkins Freeman

There were in a green field a little, low, weather-stained cottage, with a foot-path leading to it from the highway several rods distant, and two old women—one with a tin pan and old knife searching for dandelion greens among the short young grass, and the other sitting on the door-step watching her, or, rather, having the appearance of watching her.

"Air there enough for a mess, Harriét?" asked the old woman on the door-step. She accented oddly the last syllable of the Harriet, and there was a curious quality in her feeble, cracked old voice. Besides the question denoted by the arrangement of her words and the rising inflection, there was another, broader and subtler, the very essence of all questioning, in the tone of her voice itself; the cracked, quavering notes that she used reached out of themselves, and asked, and groped like fingers in the dark. One would have known by the voice that the old woman was blind.

The old woman on her knees in the grass searching for dandelions did not reply; she evidently had not heard the question. So the old woman on the doorstep, after waiting a few minutes with her head turned expectantly, asked agin, varying her question slightly, and speaking louder:

"Air there enough for a mess, do ye s'pose, Harriét?"

The old woman in the grass heard this time. She rose slowly and laboriously the effort of straightening out the rheumatic old muscles was evidently a painful one; then she eyed the greens heaped up in the tin pan, and pressed them down with her hand.

"Wa'al, I don't know, Charlotte," she replied hoarsely. "There's plenty of them here, but I ain't got near enough for a mess; they do bile down so when you et 'em in the pot; an' it's all I can do to bend my j'ints enough to dig 'em."

"I'd give consider'ble to help ye, Harriét," said the old woman on the doorstep.

But the other did not hear her; she was down on her knees in the grass again, anxiously spying out the dandelions.

So the old woman on the doorstep crossed her little shriveled hands over her calico knees, and sat quite still, with the soft spring wind blowing over her.

The old wooden doorstep was sunk low down among the grasses, and the whole house to which it belonged had an air of settling down and mouldering into the grass as into its own grave.

When Harriet Shattuck grew deaf and rheumatic, and had to give up work as tailoress, and Charlotte Shattuck lost her eyesight, and was unable to do any more sewing for her livelihood, it was a small and trifling charity for the rich man who held a mortgage on the little house in which they had been born and lived all their lives to give them the use of it, rent and interest free. He might as well have taken credit to himself for not charging a squirrel for his tenement in some old decaying tree in his woods.

So ancient was the little habitation, so wavering and mouldering, the hands that had fashioned it had lain still so long in their graves, that it almost seemed to have fallen below its distinctive rank as a house. Rain and snow had filtered through its roof, mosses had grown over it, worms had eaten it, and birds built their nests under its eaves; nature had almost completely overrun and obliterated the work of man, and taken her own to herself again, till the house seemed as much a natural ruin as and old tree stump.

The Shattucks had always been poor people and common people; no especial grace and refinement or fine ambition had ever characterized any of them; they had always been poor and coarse and common. The father and his father before him had simply lived in the poor little house, grubbed for their living, and then unquestioningly died. The mother had been of no rarer stamp, and the two daughters were cast in the same mould.

After their parents' death, Harriet and Charlotte had lived alone in the old place from youth to old age, with the one hope of ability to keep a roof over their heads, covering on their backs, and victuals in their mouths—an all-sufficient one with them.

Neither of them had ever had a lover; they had always seemed to repel rather than attract the opposite sex. It was not merely because they were poor, ordinary, and homely; there were plenty of men in the place who would have matched them well in that respect; the fault lay deeper— in their characters. Harriet, even in her girlhood, had a blunt, defiant manner that almost amounted to surliness, and was well-calculated to alarm timid adorers, and Charlotte had always had the reputation of not being any too strong in her mind.

Harriet had gone about from house to house doing tailorwork after the primitive country fashion, and Charlotte had done plain sewing and mending for the neighbors. They had been, in the main, except when pressed by some temporary anxiety about their work or the payment thereof, happy and contented, with that negative kind of happiness and contentment that comes not from gratified ambition, but a lack of ambition itself. All that they cared for they had had in tolerable abundance, for Harriet at least had been swift and capable about her work. The patched, mossy old roof had been kept over their heads, the coarse, hearty food that they loved had been set on their table, and their cheap clothes had been warm and strong.

After Charlotte's eyes failed her, and Harriet had the rheumatic fever, and the little hoard of earnings went to the doctors, times were harder with them, though still it could not be said that they actually suffered.

When they could not pay the interest on the mortgage, they were allowed to keep the place interest free; there was as much fitness in a mortgage on the little house, anyway, as there would have been on a rotten old apple tree; and the people about, who were mostly farmers, and good friendly folk, helped them out with their living. One would donate a barrel of apples from his abundant harvest to the two poor old women, one a barrel of potatoes, another a load of wood for the winter fuel, and many a farmer's wife had bustled up the narrow foot path with a pound of butter, or a dozen fresh eggs, or a nice bit of pork. Besides all this, there was a tiny garden patch behind the house, with a straggling row of currant bushes in it, and one of gooseberries, where Harriet contrived every year to raise a few pumpkins, which were the pride of her life. On the right of the garden were two old apple trees, a Baldwin and a Porter, both yet in tolerably good fruit-bearing state.

The delight that the two poor old souls took in their own pumpkins, their apples and currants, was indescribable. It was not merely that they contributed largely towards their living; they were their own, their private share of the great wealth of nature, the little taste set apart for them alone out of her bounty, and worth more to them on that account, though they were not conscious of it, than all the richer fruits that they received from their neighbors' gardens.

This morning the two apple trees were brave with flowers, the currant bushes looked alive, and the pumpkin seeds were in the ground. Harriet cast complacent glances in their direction form time to time, as she painfully dug her dandelion greens. She was a short, stoutly built old woman, with a large face coarsely wrinkled, with a suspicion of a stubble of beard on the square chin.

When her tin pan was filled to her satisfaction with the sprawling, spidery greens, and she was hobbling stiffly towards her sister on the doorstep, she saw another woman standing before her with a basket in her hand.

"Good-morning, Harriet," she said, in a loud, strident voice, as she drew near. "I've been frying some doughnuts, and I brought you over some warm."

"I've been tellin' her it was real good in her," piped Charlotte from the doorstep, with an anxious turn of her sightless face towards the sound of her sister's footstep.

Harriet said nothing but a hoarse, "Good-morning', Mis' Simonds." Then she took the basket in her hand, lifted the towel off the top, selected a doughnut, and deliberately tasted it.

"Tough," she said. "I s'posed so. If there is anything I 'spise on this airth it's a tough doughnut."

"Oh, Harriét!" said Charlotte, with a frightened look.

"They air tough," said Harriet, with hoarse defiance, "and if there is anything I 'spise on this airth it's a tough doughnut."

The woman whose benevolence and cookery were being thus ungratefully received only laughed. She was quite fleshy, and a round, rosy, determined face.

"Well, Harriet," said she, "I am sorry they are tough, but perhaps you had better take them out on a plate, and give me my basket. You may be able to eat two or three of them if they are tough."

"They air tough—turrible tough," said Harriet stubbornly; but she took the basket into the house and emptied it of its contents nevertheless.

"I suppose your roof leaked as bad as ever in that heavy rain day before yesterday?" said the visitor to Harriet, with an inquiring squint towards the mossy shingles, as she was about to leave with her empty basket.

"It was turrible," replied Harriet, with crusty acquiescence—"turrible. We had to set pails an' pans everywheres, an' move the bed out."

"Mr. Upton ought to fix it."

"There ain't any fix to it; the old ruff ain't fit to nail new shingles on to; the hammerin' would bring the whole thing down on our heads," said Harriet, grimly.

"Well, I don't know as it can be fixed, it's so old. I suppose the wind comes in bad around the windows and doors too?"

"It's like livin' with a piece of paper, or mebbe a sieve, 'twixt you an' the wind an' the rain," quoth Harriet, with a jerk of her head.

"You ought to have a more comfortable home in your old age," said the visitor thoughtfully.

"Oh, it's well enough," cried Harriet, in quick alarm, and with a complete change of tone; the woman's remark had brought an old dread over her. "The old house'll last as long as Charlotte an' me do. The rain ain't so bad, nuther is the wind; there's room enough for us in the dry places, an' out of the way of the doors an' windows. It's enough sight better than goin' on the town." Her square, defiant old face actually looked pale as she uttered the last words and stared apprehensively at the woman.

"Oh, I did not think of your doing that," she said hastily and kindly. "We all know how you feel about that, Harriet, and not one of us neighbors will see you and Charlotte go to the poorhouse while we've got a crust of bread to share with you."

Harriet's face brightened. "Thank ye, Mis' Simonds," she said with reluctant courtesy. "I'm much obleeged to you an' the neighbors. I think mebbe we'll be able to eat some of them doughnuts if they air tough," she added, mollifyingly, as her caller turned down the footpath.

"My, Harriét," said Charlotte, lifting up a weakly, wondering, peaked old face, "what did you tell her them doughnuts was tough fur?"

129

"Charlotte, do you want everybody to look down on us, an' think we ain't no account at all, just like beggars, 'cause they bring us in vittles?" said Harriet, with a grim glance at her sister's meek, unconscious face.

"No, Harriét," she whispered.

"Do you want to go to the poorhouse?"

"No, Harriét." The poor little old woman on the doorstep fairly cowered before her aggressive old sister.

"Then don't hender me agin when I tell folks their doughnuts is tough an' their pertaters is poor. If I don't kinder keep up an' show some sperrit, I sha'n't think nothing of myself, an' other folks won't nuther, and fust thing we know they'll kerry us to the poorhouse. You'd 'a been there before now if it hadn't been for me, Charlotte."

Charlotte looked meekly convinced, and her sister sat down on a chair in the doorway to scrape her dandelions.

⌒

When the two old women sat down complacently to their meal of pork and dandelion greens in their little kitchen, they did not dream how destiny slowly and surely was introducing some new colors into their web of life, even when it was almost completed, and that this was one of the last meals they would eat in their old home for many a day. In about a week from that day, they were established in the "Old Ladies' Home" in a neighboring city. It came about in this wise: Mrs. Simonds, the woman who had brought the gift of hot doughnuts, was a smart, energetic person, bent on doing good, and she did a great deal. To be sure, she always did it in her own way. If she chose to give hot doughnuts, she gave hot doughnuts; it made not the slightest difference to her if the recipients of her charity would infinitely have preferred ginger cookies. Still, a great many would like hot doughnuts, and she did unquestionably a great deal of good.

She had a worthy coadjutor in the person of a rich and childless elderly widow in the place. They had fairly entered into a partnership in good works, with about an equal capital on both sides, the widow furnishing the money and Mrs. Simonds, who had much the better head of the two, furnishing the active schemes of benevolence.

The afternoon after the doughnut episode, she had gone to the widow with a new project, and the result was the entrance fees had been paid, and old Harriet and Charlotte made sure of a comfortable home for the rest of their lives. The widow was hand in glove with officers of missionary boards and trustees of charitable institutions. There had been an unusual mortality among the inmates of the "Home" that spring. There were several vacancies, and the matter of the admission of Harriet and Charlotte was very quickly and easily arranged. But the matter that would have seemed the least difficult—inducing the two old women to accept the bounty that Providence, the widow, and Mrs. Simonds were ready to bestow on them—proved the most so. The struggle to persuade them to abandon their tottering old home for a better was a terrible one. The widow had pleaded with mild surprise, and Mrs. Simonds with benevolent determination; the counsel and reverend eloquence of the minister had been called in, and, when they yielded at last, it was with a sad grace for the recipients of a worthy charity.

It had been hard to convince them that the "Home" was not an almshouse under another name, and their yielding at length to anything short of actual force was only due probably to the plea, which was advanced most eloquently to Harriet, that Charlotte would be so much more comfortable.

The morning they came away, Charlotte cried pitifully, and trembled all over her little shriveled body. Harriet did not cry. But when her sister had passed out the low, sagging door, she turned the key in the lock, then took it out and thrust it slyly into her pocket, shaking her head to herself with an air of fierce determination.

Mrs. Simonds' husband, who was to take them to the depot, said to himself, with disloyal defiance of his wife's active charity, that it was a shame, as he helped the two distressed old souls into his light wagon, and put the poor little box with their homely clothes in behind.

Mrs. Simonds, the widow, the minister, and the gentleman from the "Home" who was to take charge of them, were all at the depot, their faces beaming with the delight of successful benevolence. But the two poor old women looked like two forlorn prisoners in their midst. It was an impressive illustration of the truth of the saying that "it is more blessed to give than to receive."

Well, Harriet and Charlotte Shattuck went to the "Old Ladies' Home" with reluctance and distress. They stayed two months, and then—they ran away.

The "Home" was comfortable, and in some respects even luxurious, but nothing suited those two unhappy, unreasonable old women.

The fare was of a finer, more delicately served variety than they had been accustomed to; those finely flavored nourishing soups, for which the "Home" took great credit to itself, failed to please palates used to common, coarser food.

"O Lord, Harriét, when I set down to the table here, there ain't no chinks" [a plant in the wintergreen family], Charlotte used to say. "If we could hev some cabbage, or some pork an' greens, how the light would stream in!"

Then they had to be more particular about their dress. They had always been tidy enough, but now it had to be something more; the widow, in the kindness of her heart, had made it possible, and the good folks in charge of the "Home," in the kindness of their hearts, tried to carry out the widow's designs.

But nothing could transform these two unpolished old women into two nice old ladies. They did not take kindly to white lace caps and delicate neckerchiefs. They liked their new black cashmere dresses well enough, but they felt as if they broke a commandment when they put them on every afternoon. They had always worn calico with long aprons at home, and they wanted to now. They wanted to twist up their scanty grey locks into little knots at the back of their heads and go without caps, just as they always had done.

Charlotte in a dainty white cap was pitiful, but Harriet was both pitiful and comical. They were totally at variance with their surrounds, and they felt it keenly, as people of their stamp always do. No amount of kindness and attention—and they had enough of both—sufficed to reconcile them to their new abode. Charlotte pleaded continually with her sister to go back to their old home.

"O, Lord, Harriét," she would exclaim (by the way, Charlotte's "O Lord," which, as she used it, was innocent enough, had been heard with much disfavor in the "Home," and she, not knowing at all why, had been remonstrated concerning it), "Let us go home. I can't stay here no ways in this world. I don't like their vittles, an' I don't like to wear a cap; I want to go home and do different. The currants will be ripe, Harriét. O, Lord, thar was almost a chink, thinking about 'em. I want some of 'em; an' the Porter apples will be gittin' ripe, an' we could have some apple pie. This here ain't good; I want merlasses fur sweeting. Can't we get back no ways, Harriét? It ain't far, an' we could walk, an' they don't lock us in, nor nothin'. I don't want to die here; it ain't so straight up to heaven from here. O, Lord, I've felt as if I was slantendicular from heaven ever since I've been here, an' it's been so awful dark. I ain't had any chinks. I want to go home, Harriét."

"We'll go tomorrow morning'," said Harriet, finally; "we'll pack up our things an' go; we'll put on our old dresses, an' we'll do up the new ones in bundles, an' we'll just shy out the back way tomorrow mornin'; an' we'll go. I kin find the way, an' I reckon we kin get thar, if it is fourteen mile. Mebbe somebody will give us a lift."

And they went. With a grim humor, Harriet hung the new white lace caps with which she and Charlotte had been so pestered, one on each post at the head of the bedstead, so they would met the eyes of the first person who opened the door. Then they took their bundles, stole shyly out, and were soon on the high road, hobbling along, holding each other's hands, as jubilant as two children, and chuckling to themselves over their escape, and the probable astonishment there would be in the "Home" over it.

"O, Lord, Harriét, what do you s'pose they will say to them caps?" cried Charlotte with a gleeful cackle.

"I guess they'll see as folks ain't goin' to be made to wear caps agin their will in a free kentry," returned Harriet with an echoing cackle as they sped feebly and bravely along.

The "Home" stood on the very outskirts of the city, luckily for them. They would have found it difficult undertaking to traverse the crowded streets. As it was, a short walk brought them into the free country road–free comparatively, for even here at ten o'clock in the morning there was considerable traveling to and from the city on business or pleasure.

People they met on the road did not stare at them as curiously as might have been expected. Harriet held her bristling chin high in the air and hobbled along with such an appearance of being well aware of what she was about that led folks to doubt their own first opinion that there was something unusual about the two old women.

Still, their evident feebleness now and then occasioned from one and another more particular scrutiny. When they had been on the road a half-hour or so, a man in a covered wagon drove up behind them. After he had passed them, he poked his head around the front of the vehicle and looked back. Finally, he stopped and waited for them to come up to him.

"Like a ride, ma'am?" said he, looking at once bewildered and compassionate.

"Thankee," said Harriet, "we'd be much obleeged."

After the man had lifted the old women into the wagon and established them on the back seat, he turned around, as he drove slowly along, and gazed at them curiously.

"Seems to me you look pretty feeble to be walking far," said he. "Where were you going?"

Harriet told him with an air of defiance.

"Why," he exclaimed, "it is fourteen miles out. You could never walk it in the world. Well, I am going within three miles of there, and I can go on a little farther as well as not. But I don't see–Have you been in the city?"

"I have been visitin' my married darter in the city," said Harriet calmly.

Charlotte started and swallowed convulsively.

Harriet had never told a deliberate falsehood before in her life, but this seemed to her one of the tremendous exigencies of life that justify a lie. She felt desperate. If she could not contrive to deceive him in some way, the man might turn directly around and carry Charlotte and her back to the "Home" and the white caps.

"I should not have thought your daughter would have let you start for such a walk as that," said the man. "Is this lady your sister? She is blind, isn't she? She does not look fit to walk a mile."

"Yes, she's my sister," replied Harriet stubbornly, "an' she's blind; an' my darter didn't want us to walk. She felt reel bad about it. But she couldn't help it. She's poor and her husband's dead, an' she's got four leetle children."

Harriet recounted the hardships of her imaginary daughter with glibness that was astonishing. Charlotte swallowed again.

"Well," said the man, "I am glad I overtook you, for I don't think you would ever have reached home alive."

About six miles from the city, an open buggy passed them swiftly. In it were seated the matron and one of the gentlemen in charge of the "Home." They never thought of looking into the covered wagon—and, indeed, one can travel in one of those vehicles, so popular in some parts of New England, with as much privacy as he could in his tomb. The two in the buggy were seriously alarmed and anxious for the safety of the old women, who were chuckling maliciously in the wagon they soon left far behind. Harriet had watched them breathlessly until they disappeared on a curve of the road; then she whispered to Charlotte.

A little after noon, the two old women crept slowly up the footpath across the field to their old home.

"The clover is up to our knees," said Harriet; "an' the sorrel and the white-weed; an' there's lots of yaller butterflies."

O, Lord, Harriét, thar's a chink, an' I do believe I saw one of them yaller butterflies go past it," cried Charlotte, trembling all over and nodding her gray head violently.

Harriet stood on the old sunken doorstep and fitted the key, which she drew triumphantly from her pocket, in the lock, while Charlotte stood waiting and shaking behind her.

Then they went in. Everything was there just as they had left it. Charlotte sank down on a chair and began to cry. Harriet hurried across to the window that looked out on the garden.

"The currants air ripe," said she; "*an'* them pumpkins hev run all over everything."

"O, Lord, Harriét," sobbed Charlotte, "thar is so many chinks that they air all runnin' together!"

Mary Eleanor Wilkins Freeman (1852-1930) is best known for her stories and novels of New England life. She wrote fiction for children as well as adults. In 1926, she was awarded a medal for distinction in fiction by the American Academy of Letters. Her literary reputation benefited from the women's liberation movement, particularly after The Feminist Press published her collection *The Revolt of Mother and Other Stories* in 1972. Another excellent portrayal of aging is her story "The Village Singer." "A Mistaken Charity" was written in 1887.

The House on Fell Street

Isabelle Maynard

The house on Fell Street stands in a row of dilapidated Victorian houses, distinguished from the others by the stocky palm tree in its front yard and a luminous blue cross on its roof. It was there, in 1956, I met Alexander Pavlovitch Pomerenko. Mr. Pomerenko lived in the basement, sharing the premises with several other recently arrived Russian refugees from China. The floor above his room housed a modest Russian Orthodox chapel tended by nuns, and the top floor was used by them as their personal quarters. Mr. Pomerenko was a double amputee–he had contracted gangrene while in a refugee camp in the Philippines.

I, too, was from China, having left with my family as the Communists neared Tientsin. Like Mr. Pomerenko, my parents had left Russia during the revolution, settled in China, where I was born, then were forced to flee again to America, where I trained to become a social worker. Since I spoke Russian, Mr. Pomerenko's case had been assigned to me. My principal task was to try to convince him to move into a nursing home, a plan devised on his behalf by my supervisor, Mrs. Marinian–a busty, assertive woman–and Father Gerasim, a meek man of God in the Russian community. I was warned that Mr. Pomerenko was stubborn and had resisted all previous efforts to move him. "You have got to be forceful with him," Mrs. Marinian said to me. "He's got to be moved because he can't take care of himself in his condition. The sores on his stumps keep getting reinfected. It's because of the filthy conditions he lived in and his awful diet." I read the last entry in his folder: "November 5, 1955. Client totally uncooperative–refused to move. Case closed."

Armed with buoyant enthusiasm and a passionate desire to be helpful, I arrived one wet February afternoon at the basement entrance to Mr.

Pomerenko's residence. I walked down a narrow path at the side of the house, scuffling through sodden leaves left unswept on the pavement. The door was ajar, and the rain slanting in had left a puddle by the doorsill. It was quiet in the hallway. I saw several closed doors, none bearing numbers or names. A single naked bulb hung from the ceiling, giving off a flickering light. "Mr. Pomerenko," I yelled, "where are you?"

First there was silence, then a cough, then a gravelly voice: "I'm here, first door to your right." I found myself in a room so tiny that, from the center, I could almost have reached all four walls with my outstretched hands. A desk piled high with newspapers and magazines stood against one wall; two of the other walls had shelves from floor to ceiling filled with books. A green gooseneck lamp on a small wooden table gave off a weak light; the only other light came from a narrow window with streaky panes.

Mr. Pomerenko lay on a low bed covered with a worn satin quilt. Piled high on the bed in total disarray were books, notepads, pencils, boxes, balls of string, cigarettes, coffee cups, and plates with leftover food. There was a pervading smell of dust, dampness and urine. I began to make mental notes of the various things that needed immediate change— a hospital bed to start with, daily attendant, and a move to a nursing home as soon as possible.

"Did you get my letter—to let you know I was coming?" I asked.

Mr. Pomerenko began rummaging among various papers on his bed and finally found the letter. Adjusting his pince-nez on his bony nose, he read it out loud: "Dear Mr. Pomerenko, I am a social worker from the Belding Center and have been asked by a priest in your community, Father Gerasim, to look in on you and offer you whatever services you may need. P.S.: I speak Russian."

"So, what shall we speak, dear lady social worker, English or Russian?"

"Whatever is most convenient for you."

"Let us speak both, then. You can practice your Russian, and I will practice my English. We will be mutually beneficial to each. Agreed?"

Not waiting for my reply, Mr. Pomerenko looked at the letter again and, shaking his head, said, "And what services, my dear lady, can you offer me?"

"Well, we could get you a hospital bed. Meals on Wheels and nursing care or an attendant. We could even get you into a nursing home. And it would all be free." I looked at him to see his reaction to "nursing home," but he had lowered his eyes.

"What a wonderful country this is, providing all these services to us poor, homeless refugees. First they take us in—even the legless ones like me—and now they want to take care of us. And Father Gerasim—he has become truly Americanized—a real *Amerkanetz*—to be able to get such 'services' for me."

Mr. Pomerenko leaned back on his pillow, took off his pince-nez and closed his eyes. I took this opportunity to get a good look at him. I saw a deeply lined face with grizzled, unkempt beard—the skin pale, almost yellow, but the lips full, red, and sensuous. He was dressed in pajamas, which were buttoned unevenly and bunched up at his neck. I followed his body downward with my eyes, trying to figure out where it ended, but could not because of all the objects strewn on the quilt. I wonder if he does that on purpose, I thought, in order not to draw attention to his body. At that moment, Mr. Pomerenko woke up from his catnap and with remarkable energy yelled, "Trying to figure out where I end, aren't you?—they all do. Well, you won't. And besides that, I don't need any of your services, so you can go back to your superiors and thank them for me. Have everything I need right here—my books, my cigarettes, my lovely neighbors, my soft bed, and my view of the calla lilies." He pointed to the window, and I realized that from his bed he could see a group of the milky white lilies under an elm tree.

"Maybe I can just come back and talk."

"Well, I can always talk. Matter of fact, wouldn't be bad talking to a pretty lady like you. Get Mrs. Berezina down the hall all excited and jealous. Good for my reputation. Yes, you can come and talk. But no social work talk. No nursing home talk. Well, now that we are going to talk, what shall I call you? You can call me Alexander Pavlovitch."

No one had ever called me by my patronymic. "My given name is Isabelle, and my father's is Abraham."

Mr. Pomerenko closed his eyes and was quiet for a few moments. "I've got it. I'll call you Isolda Abramovna. Close enough to Isabelle, and I once had a love named Isolda. But enough for now. *Do Vstretchi*—till we meet again." He closed his eyes, sank deep into his bed and turned off the light. The interview was over.

My supervisor felt I had not been assertive enough. "He'll manipulate you and sweet-talk you, just as he has others. You have got to take the bull by the horns and work on him to accept the reality of his situation. We have to get him into a nursing home–fast." I pointed out to her that I needed to get to know him before I could start convincing him of the merits of nursing homes. I needed time, I said. My supervisor was skeptical.

I arrived for my next appointment at a pre-arranged time. Mr. Pomerenko was asleep, and the room looked even messier than before. It was cluttered with plates with leftover, dried food on the floor, and a Sunday newspaper spread all over the bed. Two bags of garbage, tied with a red string, stood by the door. The gooseneck lamp cast a greenish light on his face. He stirred slightly but kept on sleeping. He's pretending, I thought. Well, old buzzard, I am not giving up. I've got patience. I sat down on the only available chair and began to read the paper. fifteen minutes went by. I heard Mr. Pomerenko clear his throat.

"Well, well, it is Isolda Abramovna. Welcome. So this is the day for our talk. And how is the world outside? Mrs. Berezina, that wicked lady next door who comes in to peek at my body, tells me the sun is out and the roses are blooming. Is that true, *dyshenka*? That means 'little soul.' I would go out and see for myself–the spirit is willing, but this body has betrayed me."

"It *is* sunny outside, and the roses *are* blooming. Shall I pick you a few?"

"The nuns won't like it. But let's do it anyway. It will drive poor Mrs. Berezina crazy when she sees her competition bringing flowers."

Mr. Pomerenko began to guffaw with great glee at his own words. The whole bed swayed as his body shook with laughter, and several books and notepads slid off the quilt. As I started to pick them up from the floor, Mr. Pomerenko said, "You don't have to do that. Paul will do it tomorrow–he comes twice a week to help, and if you do it he won't have anything to do. Wonderful boy. Met him in the camp in the Philippines after I had my surgery. He had no parents. I had no one. We sort of gravitated toward each other—two lost souls. Now I pay him to take care of me."

"That's what I've come to talk to you about," I said. "There are so many things we could do for you to make you more comfortable. You could have an attendant every day instead of twice a week, and you wouldn't have to pay out of your own money."

Mr. Pomerenko sighed and said, "I thought we agreed—no social work talk." Seeing my crestfallen face, he went on with great patience, telling me he would rather have a countryman than a stranger take care of him. "And anyway, *dyshenka*, it is good to pay for what one gets. I like feeling rich, and Paul likes getting paid. We have a perfect system."

"But he is not a certified nurse and probably doesn't have any medical training. And you have a serious condition. You need the best professional help. How do you … uh … go?" I hesitated, embarrassed.

Mr. Pomerenko looked at me intently and began to search for something on his quilt. "I'm looking for my *pince-nez*—can you see them?" I found them wedged between two books. Mr. Pomerenko put them on carefully and stared at me for a long time. When his assessment was over, he leaned back on his pillow and said, "You are such a serious lady, my dear Isolda Abramovna. So very serious. You should smile. Laugh."

I smiled, feeling childish and silly and wondering what Mrs. Marinian would say if she saw me. No doubt she would take the case away from me.

"The matter you referred to a few minutes ago—the delicate matter, my dear lady, is taken care of by the nuns. Those angels upstairs. So not to worry. And, by the way, you have charming dimples when you smile. Very attractive."

"We are not here to talk about me, Mr. Pomerenko. We are here to talk about you." I could feel him keeping me off balance, trying to steer away from the things that needed to be talked about, just as my supervisor had warned me he would.

Mr. Pomerenko, in his most seductive, mellifluous voice, said, "Well, let's talk about me. Where shall we start?"

I was prepared. I had several brochures from the public health department and gaudy leaflets displaying hospital beds and wheelchairs. I had brochures of nursing homes showing smiling seniors attended by well-starched nurses. Mr. Pomerenko listened to me politely, took my brochures, and spent several moments studying them. "Why can't they write good prose?" he said wearily. "Leave them with me, and I will look them over." He closed his eyes, and I knew I was dismissed.

Just as I was about to leave, Mr. Pomerenko said, "Do you ever read Bialik, Tolstoy, or Thomas Mann?" I turned around. His eyes were still closed, but a smile played about his mouth. "Marvelous writers–they have soul–Russian soul."

"Not Thomas Mann–he's Teutonic," I said, pleased at being able to show off my literary knowledge.

"Maybe, *dyshenka*, maybe. But no matter. It is nice to talk to a literary woman. Mrs. Berezina only reads the local Russian newspaper. Have you ever read *Oblomov*? It's one of my favorite books. I, too, like Oblomov, have a hard time getting out of bed. Only difference is that I have no valet and no legs, although I do have Paul. *Stranaya dzizin*–what a strange life. Well, we'll talk more about Oblomov next time. And I will read your brochures. Now, how about bringing me the rose you promised?"

I walked out into the back yard and cut a full-blossomed burgundy rose. "Such beauty," murmured Mr. Pomerenko, as he held the petals against his grizzly beard.

Several weeks later, I was accosted by a tall, loose-jointed woman in front of Mr. Pomerenko's room. Although it was quite warm outside, she was dressed in many layers of clothing, and her body seemed to be in perpetual motion. She motioned me to her room (though there was no one around), in a conspiratorial manner, where she proceeded to tell me that something had to be done with Mr. Pomerenko. "It's those disgusting cigarettes he smokes. He fell asleep and could have burned down the whole building. It was Sister Antonia who smelled something burning and ran down to put out the cigarette. He's going to burn all of us–he's a maniac. And have you seen his garbage? We're going to die either from the fire or the stench. You have to get him out of here."

I charged into Mr. Pomerenko's bedroom in my most assertive manner. "Mr. Pomerenko," I announced, "the time has come for us to talk about the reality of your situation and the conditions you live in."

Mr. Pomerenko looked up from the book he was reading. "And what is reality, my dear Isolda Abramovna?"

"The reality is that you need to be in a nursing home. It is filthy here and a fire hazard. You need professional medical attention."

"Never trust professionals. They lose their hearts in their training. Sit down, my dear Isolda Abramovna, make yourself comfortable. This is your fourth visit here, and you still keep trying to sell me things I don't want. Let's just continue our lovely conversations about life, literature, and that wicked Mrs. Berezina next door."

I sat down, feeling helpless. Mr. Pomerenko, in his most charming manner, pointed to his book.

"Ah, Dostoevsky! What a writer! *Crime and Punishment*. Such characterization! Such prose! Some people deserve to die–don't you think? Those who are parasites. Take, for example, our friend Mrs. Berezina–she no doubt has been filling your head with falsehood and lies about me. Had I the power to get out of this bed, I would slit her throat."

At this point, Mr. Pomerenko made a very graphic gesture with his hand against his throat. "But I suppose she has as much right to live as I do. Or does she? Ah, the mercy and generosity of the American government! They do not discriminate–they help all. Perhaps, my dear Isolda Abramovna, you should concentrate your worthy efforts on helping poor Mrs. Berezina. I am sure she would be receptive to your services."

"You're getting off the subject, Mr. Pomerenko," I said. "I need to talk to you about your situation. You could have burned to death. We must either get you a daily attendant, or you must seriously consider a nursing home."

"*Dyshenka*, you continue to be so serious all the time. What is a little fire in the bed? I have so little fire in the heart now, I must have some in bed." Mr. Pomerenko chuckled at his joke and winked at me.

For the next hour, I continued to barrage Mr. Pomerenko with all the rational reasons why he needed help. Mr. Pomerenko persisted in teasing, charming, and diverting me with jokes and stories about Mrs. Berezina. At the end, we were both exhausted. I sat slumped in my chair, feeling a total failure. Mr. Pomerenko lay quietly, his head turned away from me toward the wall.

"I tell you what, my dear lady social worker. I know you have a full heart and good intentions. And I know you are trying to help and are feeling frustrated. Let's make a deal. I will accept a wheelchair if you stop trying to convince me to go to a nursing home, or to accept all those wonderful services 'for your own good,' as you say."

"Wonderful! I'll get you a wheelchair next week. And I'll be here for our weekly visit–with the wheelchair and a nurse to show you how to operate it."

"Such a waste of money. I was an engineer once–should be able to operate a wheelchair."

I was adamant about the nurse. Feeling a surge of success, I was now determined to bring in reinforcements–a nurse who would echo my plan and thus convince Mr. Pomerenko to go to a nursing home. Or, at the very least, perhaps impress him with a need for better hygiene.

Louise Phelps, the public health nurse, and I arrived the following week with a shiny wheelchair. With the help of Mrs. Berezina, who quite coquettishly offered to help us put Mr. Pomerenko in his chair ("She likes to see my stumps," he growled in my ear), we got him into the chair and wheeled him out into the yard.

Mr. Pomerenko was ecstatic. "You have opened up a new world for me, Isolda Abramovna. I now will make friends again with the sky and the greenery and even the snails and the bugs. Reminds me of my childhood in Russsia."

Louise Phelps was horrified at his housing arrangement, saying the place was a fire hazard and she had to report it to the Fire Department. She snooped around the basement looking for fire extinguishers, shook her head over the poor ventilation, pointed out that a man in Mr. Pomerenko's condition should not be smoking, said that his bandages needed to be changed daily and that his bedsores required prompt medical care.

"Why do you live here?" she demanded of Mr. Pomerenko. I had never allowed myself to be so blunt with him; I held my breath, waiting for his answer.

Mr. Pomerenko casually lit a cigarette, blew a few smoke rings in the direction of Louise Phelps, and said, "Actually, it's because of the singing upstairs."

"Singing?" repeated Louise Phelps, and glanced at me with a look that said Mr. Pomerenko was certifiably crazy and we needed to get him out of there as soon as possible.

"Yes, the nuns sing three times a day. Their voices, the familiar tunes, make me feel at home. Wonderful for the soul. When my soul feels empty, I remind myself that in a few hours I will hear the music seeping through the ceiling, and I feel better. Refreshed. Heavenly music," said Mr. Pomerenko, pointing up toward the chapel on the first floor.

"Stuff and nonsense," said Louise Phelps, when we left the basement apartment. "What he needs is three square meals a day, someone to give him a daily bath–did you notice the awful smell in there?–leftover food and body odor–someone to bandage his sores and make sure he takes his meds. Mark my words, that whole building will go up in flames, the way he smokes in bed. Soul, indeed! Romantic crap!

Somehow, in the presence of Louise, I found myself defending Mr. Pomerenko. "You've got to understand his cultural background. He's a proud, independent man. And he's comfortable here. Do we really have the right to make him change?"

"We have the responsibility. He is a danger to himself and others."

When I came to visit Mr. Pomerenko several weeks later, I was met by the hysterical Mrs. Berezina, in her usual three layers of clothing, gesticulating wildly and incoherently, and moaning, "I knew this would happen. If only he had listened to you." What had happened, I gathered, was that Mr. Pomerenko had had a high fever and severe bedsores and that the Russian physician, Dr. Volkoff, had called an ambulance to take him to St. Agnes' Hospital. Mrs. Berezina told me she was caring for Mr. Pomerenko's room and that she would make sure none of his things were stolen. "My wash always gets stolen," she whispered. "Only last week two pairs of my very best silk panties were taken off the line. I suspect Mrs. Vinograd, but she is sly, and I never catch her. I have tried to tell the nuns, but they are too busy praying." Mrs. Berezina began to weep and wondered if I could look into the matter. I assured her that I would do what I could at a later time.

I found Mr. Pomerenko in the corner bed of Ward B at St. Agnes' Hospital. His bed was a jungle of books and notepapers, Russian newspapers and cigarettes. "Get me out of here, my dear *dyshenka*," he said cheerfully. "This is not a house for curing people. They are trying to kill me. Imagine, they put ice cubes in the drinking water and keep the windows open all night so there is a terrible draft all the time. Americans! What do they know about health? A fine people. A kind people, generous. But drafts and ice cubes in a hospital! And all those boiled vegetables. I would give ten years of my life for one deliciously fried *pirog* with meat." I left the hospital with the promise to smuggle in some Russian food.

After a week's stay at the hospital ("Under a sun lamp, with my rear end up to dry out my bedsores," he groaned), Mr. Pomerenko came home to the house on Fell Street. Mrs. Berezina met me on the front steps, pointed with a dramatic flourish toward his room, and said, "Mind my words, he'll burn this place up–he should never have come back." Mr. Pomerenko was obviously pleased to see me and gladly accepted the bag of Russian cookies I brought for him. He told me how delighted he was to be back among his own things and how grateful he was to the American government for taking care of him in the hospital. I looked around at the messy room, with its bags of garbage, and thought of Mr. Pomerenko eating his cold meals on the days when Paul was not around to heat them up on the communal stove. I made one more effort to sell Mr. Pomerenko on the idea of Meals on Wheels and the services of a public health nurse. I even made a feeble effort to get him to accept regular checkups. I could hear my supervisor's voice saying, "You've got to work on his resistance. You're giving up too soon. You have to get him to accept what is good for him."

"No offense meant, my dear Isolda Abramovna," he said, "but warmed-up American food on plastic trays is not my cup of tea. I know Mrs. Berezina gets her meals that way, and I have seen the meals–all very uninteresting. As for checkups–what is there to check up? If I am well, there is no need to check me up. If I am sick, I will call Dr. Volkoff. He has known me for years, and once, briefly, I was married to his sister. So we are practically family. And if all your public health nurses are like Madame Louise Phelps, they can stay at home. She's too cold, too organized. Anyway, I have Paul, and he takes care of me–gives me a bath and takes care of other unpleasant personal problems. So what if I have to pay him out of my own money? It makes me feel important. The only thing I get free is the nuns' singing. Every day when they sing, I am transported back to my homeland and memories of my childhood. Where else could I get that? So, come and visit me, Isolda Abramovna, but let's not talk of 'services.'"

I stopped making regular visits, realizing that I liked Mr. Pomerenko just as he was. Besides, he did not really need me, and Mrs. Berezina was getting too demanding. Her preoccupation with missing laundry was tedious; anyway, it was a problem I couldn't do much about. I tried organizing the women into a washing day schedule, but no one wanted to participate. When I passed Mr. Pomerenko's room, he would wave to me and ask how I was. Sometimes I would bring him a rose. Often he would beckon me in to tell me about a book he was reading. We stopped discussing his health or condition. Occasionally we would share a pirog I had brought from the Russian bakery. Mr. Pomerenko always insisted we use his two flowered plates. "No plastic, no Meals on Wheels," he would smile, then wink at me. At the end of each visit, he would point a finger towards the ceiling and whisper, "That's where my soul finds solace. Do not worry about me, *dyshenka*. As long as there is music, Pomerenko lives."

Isabelle Maynard is a retired social worker whose memoir *China Dreams: Growing up Jewish in Tientsin* was published by the University of Iowa Press in 1996. Her stories have been widely published and her play *Hard Choices* has been performed in both Russian and English at Jewish community centers. Maynard's art work has been exhibited at Jack London Square in Oakland and at the Creative Aging exhibit in Washington, DC. In 2003, she received a grant from Poets and Writers.

The Blessing of Solomon

Irene Paull

Since Solomon moved away from Newton Avenue, he had nothing to tie him to the living world but the Yiddish paper. He would wait for the mailman, standing at the picture window, straining his eyes toward Summit Boulevard.

The house he lived in was set back deep in the foliage, and the trained hand of the city's best landscape gardener had conspired with good fortune to rob him of even this meagre contact with the world. Even if he could have seen out upon the road, what was there to see on Summit Boulevard? The flash of cars–he could not even distinguish the faces of their drivers. The gleam of headlights at night. The musical honk of the fine automobiles. Sometimes the screech of a brake sudden as a scream. Yet, even so, little was better than nothing.

This house was the very latest in houses. Designed as if to spite him. In the back was something they called a "patio." It looked out upon the impersonal silence of a wooded lot. Why couldn't this have been a front porch where he could sit and smoke the sweet cigarettes he rolled by hand and at least hear the world go by on Summit Boulevard? For the same reason, he thought, with a touch of irony, that when you can afford mink, you do not wear Hudson seal, and when you drive a Cadillac, it is a shame to be seen behind the wheel of a Buick, and when you have grown rich enough to live on Summit Boulevard, what fool would dream of spending his remaining years on Newton Avenue?

He recalled that it was the year Rose's husband, Ben, opened his fourth surplus store that he had taken leave of Newton Avenue. Taken leave forever of his friends, the delicatessen, the tailor shop, the fish market, the butcher shop, the synagogue. It was like taking leave of one's native village and going to spend your remaining days in a foreign land, among strangers where you would never hear your mother tongue, the sound of Yiddish, a language that melts in your mouth, a language salty as herring, warm as your mother's home-baked bread.

Mendel the tailor, his oldest friend, had tried to console him.

"Solomon," he said, "you are a man truly blessed. How many children are there nowadays who would put up with an old man? It's not like the olden times when they had respect for a father. Now they pack him off to an old people's home and they're rid of him. Do your children send you to the old people's home? God forbid!"

"God forbid!" nodded Solomon.

It was almost a year before he saw Mendel again. What maneuvering had gone into the arrangements for Mendel to visit him at Summit Boulevard! How long it had taken to summon up courage to approach his grandchildren for this favor! For the bus stop was two miles from this exclusive neighborhood. To come without a car one would have to stop at the drug store at the end of the busline and call the house, and someone would drive out in a car to pick you up. It was hard to ask a favor of your children and grandchildren when, after all, you were a guest in their house. So he waited for an opportunity to approach the matter indirectly.

It came the day Sandra was holding forth over her shorty coat.

"I told you, Mom, not to buy stuff at bargain sales! This is no shorty coat."

"It is a shorty coat."

"It's not a shorty coat. It is a three-quarter coat. A shorty coat comes to here. Like this. It's smart looking. This hangs down ... look how far it hangs ... it's tacky. And you can't return it because you got it on sale. Honest, I'm so tee'd off, I could give it to the Goodwill."

"You can cut it down," Rose suggested.

"Cut it down? Who's going to cut it down?"

Solomon saw his opportunity and interposed gently, "There's a tailor ... you know him ... Mendel on Newton Avenue near the shoemaker? He's a good tailor ... hands like gold. He makes coats for even stylish ladies. He can cut it down for you. It will look like a new coat."

Rose brightened and looked at her father with a gleam of interest.

"You mean I'm going to go traipsing way across town to some old tailor on Newton Avenue?" shrilled Sandra.

"No, no," rushed in Solomon. "God forbid. Why should you go there? He will be glad to come here and take the measurements. Business is not so rushing with him. Maybe he can close up the shop for an afternoon."

"Sometimes a tailor can do a better job than a dressmaker," Rose persisted, "especially a coat. That's their business. Coats, suits …"

The old man nodded, his eyes planted eagerly on Sandra's face.

"I will not go to some shmo of a tailor," she summarized, "and that's that. I'll take it to the alteration department at Lingaman's."

"It will cost you more than the whole coat," Rose grumbled.

"Let it cost," Sandra shot back. "Next time you won't do me any favors buying me bargains."

Solomon was defeated, but the next time he employed a direct approach.

"Dovidel," he ventured, "you're going some place Wednesday?"

"What's going on Wednesday, Gramp?" asked David.

"Nothing. I thought maybe you'd be home about two o'clock?"

"Why? What's doing?"

"What do you want, Pa?" asked Rose.

"Mendel the tailor, you remember him . . he has a little shop on Newton Avenue by the shoemaker? He would like to come and visit me maybe Wednesday. But there is nobody of course to drive him here from the bus."

"Swell idea!" David cried warmly. "You haven't got any friends your own age here. I sure would do it, Gramp, but I'm going to a ball game. Sandy can hang around here Wednesday and pick the old man up."

"What do you mean *I* can hang around?" Sandra whined, flashing her brother a murderous look. Then she turned to her grandfather and kissed him lightly on the forehead. "I'm sorry, Grandpa. I'd do it, but I've got an appointment at the beauty parlor at half past two."

"It wouldn't kill you to do the old man a favor," David said.

"Listen to that! It wouldn't kill *me*! What about *you*?"

"Shut up," cried Rose. She turned irritably to her father. "It's gotta be Wednesday?"

"Wednesday. Thursday. It doesn't matter."

"Well, let him come Thursday. But one o'clock sharp. I'll pick him up and bring him here before I go to my bridge club. Then I can drive him to the bus when I get back. But let him be at the bus stop one o'clock sharp. I can't wait around."

"One o'clock sharp," the old man nodded.

For days Solomon rehearsed in his mind the conversation he would have with Mendel. A thousand things there were to talk about. If only he could remember them. Besides the headlines in the Yiddish paper, there were the anecdotes and the thoughts about life that occurred to him from time to time. But they melted like snow in his mind because there was no one to hear them. Like youth and age. He must tell Mendel how it occurred to him as he stood looking out toward Summit Boulevard just the other day that youth looks out upon life from one wide open door, and age from a thousand bolted windows. This he must tell Mendel before it too melted away. Not that it was important. But a man liked to exchange his thoughts.

There was so much happening in the world. You had to talk to somebody. What about Nasser, for instance? And what will come of all this business with sputniks and bomb tests and what not? But with the family you couldn't exchange a word. As if it were not their world. Ben … what could you say to Ben? He knew about nothing but surplus stores. Rose had her bridge club. Sandra was interested in God knows what, and David … that was truly the most baffling thing of all.

When David was fifteen, Solomon, rummaging in the attic among his books, came upon the boy setting up a chemistry experiment. He looked startled and shamefaced at the sight of his grandfather. Misunderstanding his embarrassment, Solomon reassured him: "You do not have to be afraid that your grandfather does not understand what you are doing. In English I am ignorant, but in Yiddish I am an educated man. In the old country, they called me 'the philosopher.' I know little of science, but my interest is great."

David was sheepish. "Don't tell anybody about this, will you, Grandpa?"

"Who should I tell?" shrugged the old man.

"The folks know I'm pretty good at this stuff. If they think I'm too interested, they'll get on my neck to try out for one of those science prizes. They're already bothering me about it."

"So what is so terrible? Maybe you would win one?"

"That's just it. You don't understand, Gramps. You win a thing like that … it gets around … the kids think you're a brain."

"A brain? What's a brain?"

"Brains …" David tapped his head. "You know … brains …"

"That's bad … brains?" puzzled the old man. "What can be wrong with having brains?"

"Oh, you don't understand. I can't explain it … they think you're nuts … different … it's just funny, that's all."

Solomon spread his hands in bewilderment.

"A funny thing the world has come to, a Jewish boy should be afraid of having brains," he was muttering to himself as he clumped cautiously down the attic stairs.

Solomon pondered many times in his life how you wait and wait for some particular event. You exhaust endless days in waiting and anticipation. And, suddenly, it happens, and, just as suddenly, it is over and you are looking back upon it, pondering the nature of time and the brevity of life.

He had wished away a week of his life, living for nothing but Mendel's coming, and at last the waiting was over, and Mendel was there! Mendel came dressed in the shiny broadcloth suit he wore only on the high holidays. He sat on the edge of the satin chair, afraid to touch its pale arms with his hands or his elbows.

"And how is business?" asked Solomon.

"One lives," Mendel replied absently, a trapped look on his face, as if he were smothering in the room's lush opulence. "This is certainly a fine house," he added, politely, "a house like this must cost a man a fortune."

"How's Leah and the grandchildren?"

"All well, thank God," Mendel replied, still absently. "The taxes alone on a house like this a poor man could live on for half a year."

"And Sam Elman, he is better?"

"What better? From such a sickness, who recovers? God lives and the people suffer." He looked down at his feet. White rugs. Deep as an inch of snow. He wondered with a sudden stop of his breath if he had stepped on freshly tarred street on Newton Avenue.

"Maybe you would like a smoke, Mendel?"

Mendel declined with alarm.

More questions, briefly answered.

"Come, let us go sit in the kitchen," said Solomon.

"Aha!" cried Mendel, rising quickly with a grateful smile. "That is really a good idea!" But, before moving from the spot, he carefully examined the soles of his shoes.

"We could sit outside," sighed Solomon, "but, to spite us, it's drizzling. Such a weather we have. Two seasons. Winter and July."

"The kitchen is very good," said Mendel, still smiling. "What could be better than a kitchen? It will be like old times."

His smile vanished as Solomon led him into the kitchen—a cold marriage of stainless steel and dazzling porcelain. "Like an operating room" thought Mendel with a shudder, his eyes casting about for the kitchen table.

"There is a button somewhere," said Solomon. "You press a button and a table comes out of the wall." He pressed the wrong button, and an ironing board leaped out at Mendel. He sprang back, trembling. Solomon pressed another button and a shelf began revolving.

"So, who needs a table?" said Mendel, trying to put his distracted host at ease.

"Some place there is a button," said Solomon doggedly.

He finally found it, and they sat down together at the narrow little utility table of gleaming white formica. It scarcely resembled a kitchen table. They felt awkward and ill at ease.

Solomon rose. He wanted to serve his friend a glass of tea. He fumbled about the shelves and realized that he didn't know where to look for anything. It was the maid's day off.

"Forget the tea," said Mendel, sympathetically. "Who's thirsty?"

But one doesn't entertain a guest and serve him nothing. Solomon found some fresh peaches in the refrigerator. They ate them in silence, slowly, almost as if to postpone the need for conversation. Then Mendel looked on with discomfiture as Solomon thrashed about for some place to dispose of the peelings and the peach stones. Where was the garbage pail? In some hole in the wall no doubt, and only God knows where they have hidden the button. Defeated, he rolled the refuse into a scrap of Yiddish paper and stuffed it into his pocket.

At last Rose came home from her bridge game to drive Mendel to the station.

When it came time to part, they did not meet each other's eyes. They stood bleakly a moment, like two gnarled trees, numbed by the biting frost of December.

The Mendel said in their beloved Yiddish, "Nu, be well."

"Go well," said Solomon.

"May we live, please God, to meet again."

Solomon shrugged. "The Lord is merciful. The greatest compensation in this life is that He does not compel a man to live forever."

It was another Friday night. A Sabbath eve. The family had all gone their separate ways, and Solomon was musing to himself. He remembered with nostalgia that, about this time of night, the Sabbath service would be over in the synagogue, and familiar friends would be gathering on the stone stairs to exchange a story, a bit of gossip, or a serious comment on the day's headlines. Then they would walk together slowly through the perfumed evening, sweet with pine and rustling apple blossoms. "But Mendel is right," he thought. "How many children are there nowadays who would put up with an old father? They'd pack him off to an old people's home and be rid of him. After all, he had his own ways."

That evening, he overheard Rose on the telephone talking to his son, Irving.

"Irv," she said, "it wouldn't hurt you to come over and take Pa for a ride once in a while or drop in for a game of pinochle or something. So you're busy, who isn't? After all, he was a good father. He did the best he could. A man can't sit all day like a dummy talking to the wall. After all, Ben's only a son-in-law. Say, he's pretty good as it is. After all, it's not his father. Never mind you're busy, Irv. He's not going to live forever. After he's gone, it'll be too late to say you're sorry. You hear me, Irv?"

"She has a big mouth but also a big heart," thought Solomon sadly.

He did not want to overhear Rose's telephone conversations, but her voice was loud and carried to the patio. The day before, he had heard her talking.

"Listen," she had said, "he's not so young … he's seventy-one, God bless him. I should look so good at his age. What should I do with an old father … send him to the old people's home? But what are you going to do? They've got their own ways. It's an aggravation, but you've got to put up with it. What do you mean old age pension? You think it's the money? How could I let an old man like that stay alone in a room some place … he can't even boil water for himself. And what if he should slip on the ice or something? What would people say? They get on your nerves, sure, but what are you going to do. Sick, what sick? A little of this, a little of that. He can't do much walking, but I should feel so good at seventy-one. So you have a few aches and pains. Say, when you get old, what do you expect? An appetite he's got, thank God."

Solomon thought for a long time about what he had overheard. He thought deeply. Then, as if someone were shouting at him, he heard a question: *What is wrong with the old people's home?*

Why have I been so fearful of the old people's home, he thought. Didn't the wise rabbi say never look upon tomorrow with yesterday's eyes? An old people's home was not a poorhouse. It was not like the olden times. Why should it be so dreaded? There I would find other people like myself. My own generation. Somebody to talk with. To exchange thoughts. To discuss the day's news. To walk with a little. To trade a joke. Here I am a dry, black stalk in a freshly planted vineyard. There how happily I could live out my years! They say Simon Frisch is in the old people's home. And Hyman Segal. Simon I haven't seen in three years. A *schlimzel* he always was. But he could tell a story to split your side. Hyman, it's true, was a bit of a *noodnik*, but even a *noodnik* is better than nobody.

For the first time since he left Newton Avenue, he was a living man, capable of hope and joy and growth. He hummed a tune as he rummaged in his room among his few possessions. This he would take with him to the home. This he would throw away. This perhaps David would like to have as a keepsake.

Tomorrow afternoon when she was alone, he'd talk to Rose. If he could convince her that this was what he wanted, she would be happy to please him. If she could see that he really wanted to go to the old people's home, that this would be a great joy to him and that he looked upon it with anticipation, she would not deny him this happiness. The money it would cost he was sure would be no problem. They could raise the money among the children. And then, when it was all settled, think of the pleasure it would be for Rose not to have him on her hands. And Ben. After all, only a son-in-law.

He approached her the next afternoon as she prepared to leave for her Saturday shopping.

"Raisel, my dear," he said, using the familiar Yiddish.

"Yeah, Pa," she tossed off carelessly as she painted her lips in front of the mirrored wall.

"I've been thinking, Raisel. What is so bad about the old people's home?"

"What old people's home?"

"I mean an old people's home is a good idea. It's not like the old days. People don't look at it the same way."

"Old people's home? What old people's home?" snapped Rose. "What are you bothering my head with an old people's home?"

"I mean, Raisel, you can sit with people your own age … you have somebody to talk to. This is nice. A very nice thing."

"Well, so it's nice, so what?"

"So I mean, Raisel, I would like very much to go to the old people's home. This is what I would like very much. If you please."

Rose turned on him, her face pale.

"Pa, are you crazy? What would people say? That Rose Feldman sent her old father to the old people's home? What kind of crazy business is this?"

"Let them say. What do you care what they say? I have friends there. Simon Hirsch …"

"Simon Hirsch!" cried Rose. "For months they talk about Joe Hirsch–they're still talking about him for sending his father there. It was a shame. It disgraced him!"

"People have different ideas now. Things change. It is no disgrace. This is what I want, Raisel. This is what I want very much. Believe me, this would make me very happy."

"Make you happy! What about me? You want to make a fool out of me all over town? An old people's home … imagine that! I wouldn't be able to look people in the face, for God's sake!"

"But I want …"

"You want! You don't know what you want! You've got a beautiful home in the best part of town. Everybody waits on you. A maid even brings in your Yiddish paper. And you want to make a fool out of me. You're in your second childhood!"

Solomon's silent gesticulating hands dropped to his sides.

"Some people just aren't satisfied no matter what you do for them," Rose cried, almost in tears. "Old people's home!" She seized her purse and jacket. There was the clackety-clack of her high heels on the stone patio as she headed for the garage to get her car. Then loud snorting of the high-powered motor as the sleek beast burst out of the garage with a roar and rolled down the road to join the endless caravan of cars flashing faceless along the dark ribbon of Summit Boulevard.

Irene Paull (1908–1981) liked to quote Oliver Wendell Holmes, Jr. who said we are required to "share the passion and action of the time at peril of being judged not to have lived." Paull was intensely involved in struggles for justice—for the immigrant community of her youth and in movements for labor, civil rights, peace, women and seniors. *Irene: A Selection of Writings by Irene Paull*, edited by Gayla Ellis et al., was published by Midwest Villages and Voices in 1996.

Loss

A Sort of Death

Josephine Alexander

"I don't want to die in my sleep," I said to a friend who did. "I want the experience of dying, even if I cannot write about it afterward."

Well, I am now experiencing a sort of death, complete with a reincarnation into a strange new world, a reincarnation that has turned my wheel of life, so that the personality I have endured for eighty-two years is now, in my eighty-third, somewhat different in appearance and quite different in essence.

The reason for this change is a condition I encountered last February, one that has probably plagued many people, especially, but not invariably, old people, and most frequent light-complected people, possibly since the early days of *homo sapiens*. Until recently, it was vaguely described as "near blindness" or "visual impairment," but now that modern technology has provided the tools to see macula, or the back of the eye, we call it "Macular Degeneration" or, informally, "central-" or "near-vision" loss.

One day last February, I noticed that the pages of my book and my newspaper were blurred and wavy, so I bought a stronger pair of reading glasses at the dime store. They did not help, so I went to the optometrist for a new prescription. Urgently, for reading and writing are half my life, and the other half—walking and socializing—were bringing instant strain. Overnight, the depth from step to sidewalk had become blurred, as had the faces of my neighbors, friends, and relations.

I felt no anxiety at all. Why should I? My eyes had paid their dues. From childhood, I had been nearsighted and wore glasses when it was convenient. In late middle age, I had developed glaucoma, and it had yielded to treatment. At the onset of old age, cataracts dulled my world until new lenses gave me years of the best vision I had ever had. Eye

158

surgery is scary. It reminds one that the most horrifying tragedies of Western literature are about blinding–Samson, Oedipus, Lear. Still, even if it meant another operation, my excellent eye doctors at Kaiser would fix this new problem too, barely interrupting my life.

No so. The angiograph tools for photographing and diagnosing this condition are new. Only two programs of experimental treatment are now available in the entire nation–one out of my range in the East, another here in San Francisco. This was started two years ago, and I cheerfully volunteered to be a guinea pig.

First, let me tell you what the world I live in is like. It is a distorted world–buildings have no straight lines–indeed, my world has very few straight lines. Walls and windows curve in strange ways. One of the earliest movies was a German surrealistic film called *The Cabinet of Dr. Caligari*, which imaged the world of an insane man as he described it to another asylum inmate. My world looks quite as zany as his. Yet it is often quite beautiful, for all the faceless people do have eyes, hair, form, color, and instead of walking stodgily, they float. Maybe the images of angels, seraphs, and gods came from the inner vision of some of my eloquent predecessors.

Though my reborn world is often lovely, it certainly has its inconveniences. I will never read another book, and, though books on tape and magazines on disks are a welcome substitute, they just are not the same.

Now, about the treatment I have undergone–the experiences of a guinea pig and the benefits thereof:

Dr. Wayne Fung, of Pacific Medical Center, explained at my first appointment that the treatment consisted of injections of the drug Interferon. I would have to inject myself on alternate nights, might suffer any or all of a number of side effects: headaches, crippling depression, fatigue, diarrhea. I might experience no benefit. At best, my sight would not be restored, but, by arresting the hemorrhaging of the macula, the treatment would maintain what vision I had, and my peripheral vision and depth perception might even be somewhat improved.

I did suffer most of the side effects. Now that the treatments have been completed, I believe that they were indeed worthwhile. My peripheral vision is now quite good, I am able to walk alone again with pleasure, and enjoy all the activities for which walking is essential. I have talked with other patients who report equal or better benefits, without any side effects.

Now, almost a year after I lost my central vision, my life is active and healthy again.

Many people and organizations serve the visually impaired, and I have acquired useful tools—a voice activator for my computer, a video viewer for reading my printouts, mail, and sundry, and the heartening example of many, many of my visually impaired new friends.

And the personality of my reincarnation? Well, for all of my long life, I have been a vague, dreamy person, living in a clutter of books and papers and ideas, but, since I can no longer set down anything smaller than an infant without it immediately disappearing, I am perforce becoming quite organized and often tidy. I am still able to maintain my treasured independence, with considerable assistance from my daughter and my friends. The people on my TV do look rather like creatures from another planet, but they often say or do interesting things. Pouring anything into anything is hard and often messy work, and frequently when I set things down they end up on the floor, but I am learning.

Meanwhile, Dr. Fung has advised me never to go out during the daytime without protecting my eyes with wraparound tinted glasses and brimmed hats, so my reincarnation has effected a change from my casually blowing hair. A cane adds to the new image, when I remember it.

Finally, though I miss seeing many things I used to enjoy seeing, I frequently see some of the darnedest things that are not there. Yesterday, a small black bull calf appeared outside my front door. I was shocked when it stood on its hind legs, becoming my neighbor and her bike.

All the rich memories and fantasies of a long life are helpful, too, for when the scene about me is frustrating, I can close my eyes and summon up the clear images of remembered faces, and lively, long-ago scenes. And, thanks to my good peripheral vision, I still have the beautiful San Francisco sky from my western bay windows. Only the stars are lost—not the vivid sunsets and the ever-changing moon.

I am also complying as a serene guinea pig with another research project being explored nationwide. This is the inclusion in the diet of large servings of leafy green and orange vegetables, the foods richest in the vitamin believed most healthful to the eyes. I am off to the farmers' market to stock up. Think of me as a close relative of Lewis Carroll's hero, who

> *Thought he saw an elephant who was playing on a fife*
> *He looked again, and saw it was a letter from his wife.*

Josephine Alexander (1909–1991) was a journalist, photographer, and long-time Bay Area resident. In the 1950s, she led a successful campaign against the building of a nuclear power plant north of San Francisco. Her 1981 book, *America through the Eye of My Needle* (Dial Press) received widespread praise for its analysis of the power that conglomerates wield over nearly every sphere of American life. She died at age eighty-three after she was severely burned in a household accident.

Pool with Dad

When my dead father comes,
the infinite possibilities
of the dreamworld
always are set before us.
Always this insane joy
to find one another again,
and what will we do?
We go play pool. A pilgrimage
from one dark clanny bar
to the next, settling comfortably
on those red vinyl stools,
elbows up on the polished wood,
tankards of beer before us, each
hungrily watching the other's face.
You set up your shot,
wearing that old Nehru jacket,
jolly as ever. Heaven has not
painted over those old dents and dings,
the graying of everything,
your delight in a good glass of beer,
the "chock" sound of the pool cue,
the satisfying click as the balls
find easily their swift tubes
back to the land of death; the underworld
beneath the green felt. Driving away,
it is just us in the dream truck;
the old maroon Ford with the bad springs;
that cigar and hound-dog smell
the twenty years of your goneness
have not dispersed.

Nancy A. Henry

Nancy A. Henry is an attorney who has worked for twenty years in child advocacy and mental health advocacy. She is co-editor and publisher of Moon Pie Press, a poetry press in Westbrook, ME. Her poetry has been widely published in the small press.

Retrospect

Old woman–
I can see you
huddled in your
window
remembering now ancient
lovers
who are as withered
as you.
Wrapped tightly in
your shawl
your eyes no longer look
out
but only peer in.
The fragile gold frames
of your dusty glasses
are almost a shield
but not quite
and every once in a while
I can see you shiver
in a space between
memories.

Pearl Cleage

Pearl Cleage is an Atlanta-based novelist, playwright, essayist and poet. Her first novel, *What Looks Like Crazy on an Ordinary Day*, was a New York Times best-seller and an Oprah Book Club selection. Her novel *Baby Brother's Blues* (2006) was an Essence Magazine Book Club selection. She frequently collaborates with her husband, writer Zaron W. Burnett. She is the mother of a daughter, Deignan, and grandmother of Michael and Chloe.

Window Watching

Can't hold a needle,
but I've his social security,
rest my feet on red velvet.
I rock and watch, watch
the road. No sign of him
these twenty years.
On good days the sun
comes in on flood tide
through eighteen panes of glass and lace,
throws a watery double
on a side wall.
On bad days it's dead water
inside and out.
I rock and watch until
night comes in gradual
like cataracts.
Twenty years.

Jacqueline Moore

Jacqueline Moore was born in New York City and lived for many years in London. Now retired, she divides the year between Portland, Maine and the backwoods in Searsmont, where she recovers from the city. Her poems have appeared in *off our backs*, *The New Jersey Poetry Journal*, *The Beloit Poetry Journal*, *Green Mountain Review*, *Maine Times*, *Visions International*, and *The Dissident*.

Resistance Ages

Patricia Flaherty

One recent, wind-whipped Sunday afternoon I grieved the loss of the outraged idealist I one was. The newspaper called up visions of fiery campus meetings before the first gray hair crept in by my temples. Before bills piled high and lines surrounded my smile.

I always detested the American penchant for war. My previously strident protests have given way to more sedate weekly letters to the President. Once the loss of lives in an unwinnable war seemed an almost personal affront. My screams and chants echoed down Broadway. Manhattan seemed teeming with protesting students. My anger rose above the chants. As we surged ahead, voice-to-voice, body-to-body, I'd felt vivacious, urgent, and fierce.

A nagging loss stung me that Sunday as I surveyed my paltry complaint letter about America's current conflict abroad. An earnest young staffer might read my letter, but more likely the note would be logged and discarded. I suppose it wasn't truly the outrage that I missed; I thought of the rebellious mass marching, marching down towards the sea that night. What I really missed was the fervent hope murmuring beneath the shouts. We'd swaggered without protests signs, intoxicated by our power and momentary moral clarity. We'd worn a shining boastful hope that night. Hope for the future-hope for us and in us.

Now a thin ray of sunlight struggles in through my blinds and I admire the melancholy beauty of a Maine February. I page through photographs of my bold days at Barnard College. I try to connect the paltry letters I write in stolen moments to the resistance of my past. My actions now are silent, but steady, and perhaps that is enough for now. I must cook a casserole. I must pay the phone bill. There may be a time, in my future, for days of justified rage, parades of outrage. For the moment I wave from the sidewalk. My gestures are small and quiet, but they urge a new mass of young women on.

Patricia Flaherty grew up in the Boston area. She earned a B.A. from Barnard College and an M.S.W. from Smith College. In her twenties she had the good fortune to relocate to Portland, Maine. She currently works in education in the Sebago Lakes region of Maine.

Six Years After–Death of a Spouse

Lisa Asnis

For some time I have wanted to write about grief and how to cope with it. It has been six years since my husband died. I might have written earlier but somehow have had to put all my feelings into perspective first, so that I can now sit back, reflect and gather the last years to a more comfortable level.

Grief over a lost love can be the most devastating. According to the "Holmes-Rahe Scale of Stress Rating", the death of a spouse is valued at 100, way over that of divorce or marital separation, which are only 73 and 65 respectively. I mention this simply as a reference and apparently this deals only with the first 24 months of stress.

I would like to address these thoughts primarily to someone of my age, over 70 years old. I realize that all personal griefs are different, especially after talking to a number of women and men and listening to their stories, but for an older person, and especially an older woman, the shock of losing a longtime companion can be particularly hard.

Whether it is an anticipated death or a sudden one, you are never quite prepared for it. Age, of course, makes all the difference. Perhaps if you are still in your prime and if you have led an active life, the adjustment to living alone might be easier.

In my case, my husband's death did not come suddenly but was due to a long illness of Parkinson's Disease. I was his sole caretaker for many years, the last year being particularly hard on us both. I was fully aware of the eventual outcome, though some of my friends thought I was in denial. That may have been true to a certain extent as I was always hoping for some miracle drug and carried on each day with plans for the future. This, at least helped me from day to day, but I really was unprepared for the empty hollowness of the coming days, when his time came. By hollowness I mean those moments during the day when I would have shared a meal or just sat with him and talked, moments when I felt totally alone were the worst.

Here, I must add that to have had a job to go back to would have certainly kept me busy, and I actually envied anyone who had an established career; but I had also enjoyed my husband's early retirement and I was not prepared for a new life alone. But now, thinking back, I would not have exchanged that time we had together, versus easier years of grief that a career might have offered.

I had started to go back to college the last year while my husband Al was still alive. I needed the stimulation and the contact with other people. Al approved wholeheartedly and always supported me. I took only one class, making sure that someone else would be there for him for these few hours a week. This way, I could focus on something other than his illness, if only for a short time, and as an extra bonus, he could help me when he was well. My class was in drawing and as he had been a photographer and was generally artistic, he was able to help with my perspective exercises and overall design. I had fully intended to work slowly but surely and to work towards my Bachelors Degree. I needed a goal, no matter what!

A new term started a week after Al died, but I decided to continue, as if I had a job to go to. It was extremely hard the first few weeks, trying to concentrate on the lectures and the homework. This class was in 'Critical Thinking', so different from the art class I had taken before. I would tell myself that it was only for a few hours and then I could go home and be by myself—I needed this discipline which someone with a job to go back to already had.

Yes, I did have my family to talk to, and yes, they did their best to comfort me and included me in their social activities as well; however, the nights were quite another thing and these, I told myself, would become easier as time went by. Time would eventually make the memories fuzzier and gentler. What to do in the meantime? I scanned the ads in the newspaper for support groups. On second thought, however, I had never been a joiner of such groups and thought that I would just take on more classes to keep busy. By the next term, I took two classes, one, a Women's Wellness class, a subject I was very interested in. This class helped me in two ways. One, it emphasized keeping healthy, especially in times of grief. I know too many people who just give up on life, neglecting their own welfare and living in the past. It is good to grieve and to recall the past and there will be lots of time for that, but I had always lived in the present and also looked forward to the future. This philosophy became my "backbone" so to speak, my support whenever I would slip back into moping and feeling sorry for myself. There was a present and there was a future.

Strangely enough, the Women's Wellness class also helped me in another way. The students had to do field work. We could choose anything we wanted, from shelters for abused women to groups which dealt with alcohol abuse or even bereavement. I looked at the ads again, this time with an idea in mind. I decided to join a group focusing on bereavement and see if they could help me with my grief, even while it was an assignment report, and this way I would regard it as a learning experience, but could also detach myself for my paper.

After joining a group sponsored by the local hospital, I asked permission to use some of the information for my class report. I was given full permission and I also told the group that they were welcome to read my paper. The experience worked well for us all. Each person had a different story to tell. There were about ten women and one man. The man came with his wife who was grieving for the death of her mother. Most were of middle age and older, though a couple of women were quite young widows. We were able to ask questions, give our support and we could cry as well. The two women who were in charge were well prepared with boxes of Kleenex. For the most part, they just listened quietly and let us talk or exchange comments. At one point, the woman who came with her husband and who felt guilty about not having spent enough time with her mother as she had to work, talked to me about the way I was coping by going back to college for a degree. I suggested that she could take some courses together with her husband (to divert her constant introversion of self-blame). At least, I said, they have each other and should count every moment as a treasure. I wanted to add, but did not, that I would give anything to have all the moments spent apart from my husband, and be given that time now.

Some of us in this group got together in their homes and talked about the future and happier times to come. I was so glad that I had taken this step to meet other people and to enjoy their company. Support groups do help and if they do not, one has really lost nothing but maybe gained a friend or two.

I do not recommend that everyone take college courses, it's just that I had a special goal and a goal can be achieved by anyone. Also there are many college or high school courses that are not quite as demanding as aiming for a degree. I have taken courses for most of my life and hope to continue for many years to come. If you set your sights on the future and see where you want to be in, say, five years, even write it down, you can have that goal!

One other suggestion: be wary of relying too heavily on other people for support. The change in your life should be your choice and your strength to achieve harmony within yourself.

The reason it has taken me a long time to be able to live alone and by myself has something to do with a move to another state. As my only relatives are my son and daughter-in-law who planned to move, they asked if I would like to come along to be nearer to them. I opted to leave my friends and familiar surroundings. This again is strictly a personal choice and you must weigh this move carefully. The upheaval of moving to a new home, new surroundings and leaving your friends, may be an additional strain in your already unsettled life.

I had a double major at that time, Art and Writing, which kept me very busy. I was able to transfer my credits and continue with my goal at the University of Maine. My first class was in writing, which was very good for me because I had enjoyed previous writing classes very much. This writing class also included poetry, which I had only read but had never tried to write before. It was a whole new experience for me and at first I didn't know what to write about. A friend of my husband and mine had recently died and his death was very much on my mind. We had spent wonderful times together sailing and socializing. When his wife called me to tell me of his death, it came as a shock, even though I knew that he had been seriously ill, but one is never ready for that finality. I thought about it so much that I decided to write a poem, my very first, about our good times together, especially the sailing.

Strangely enough, before my first sentence emerged, I changed tactics in mid-air and started a poem about my husband. At that time, each time

I thought about him the feeling always came as a raw reminder of my loss.

The poem was much more negative than I would have liked it to be, but that was how I felt at that moment. I wrote many more poems after this one and even joined a class for the next semester which dealt only in poetry, a form I began to appreciate, especially for its ability to say so much in such few words. After I wrote the poem about my husband, the poem seemed to help somewhat in putting my feelings to rest. Sometimes writing your thoughts on paper can release that pent-up emotion and that can be freeing. No longer do you have it only in your head, but you can refer to it anytime you wish–quite a powerful feeling I think.

Yes, time does help. Also, taking the time to rest, meditate and giving yourself moments to have fun and relax. A strong sense of humor and the ability to laugh at oneself have always helped me to get over difficult times. What I miss the most is the companionship and in particular the sharing of the day's events. These were the best parts of a life together.

One could say that those who never were in this situation can save themselves some grief, but I am happy that I can grieve. Once, soon after Al died, I complained to my son that I would not hurt so much if only Al had been even a little bit of a "bastard", to which he replied, "But then you would not have had such a good life!"

Lisa Asnis is currently working on an M.A. at the University of Maine. She concentrates on writing and literature classes, taking one per semester so that she has time for her hobbies, family, pets, friends, and walks on the beach. A short story and a poem by Asnis were published in *The Maine Review, 2001*.

Humor

Postscript

I gave my life to learning how to live.
Now that I have organized it all, now that
I have finally found out how to keep my clothes
In order, when to wash and when to sew, how
To control my glands and sexual impulses,
How to raise a family, which friends to get
Rid of and which to be loyal to, who
Is phony and who is true, how to get rid of
Ambition and how to be thrifty, now that I have
Finally learned how to be closer to the nude
And secret silence, my life
Is just about over.

Sandra Hochman

Sandra Hochman a graduate of Bennington, studied at Columbia and the Sorbonne. Her first book, *Manhattan Pastures*, won the Yale Younger Poets award. "Postscript" was published in Hochman's book *Earthworks* in 1970. Her 1972 documentary *Year of the Woman* was released in 2004.

On Life, Death, and My Cadaver

Josephine Alexander

Some years ago, I willed my body to a medical college to help its teaching staff and students advance the cause of science.

One of my contemporaries was shocked. She said she had once had to watch medical students dissecting, cracking jokes over the cadavers as they worked. But I said I liked the thought of providing my juniors with a final joke.

I was not greatly concerned at the three provisos to acceptance: (1) No pickup service should I die inconveniently far away; (2) or obese; or (3) or by incineration.

Well, those were problems I would just have to meet when the time came, but the most pressing problem was that medical schools have an embarrassment of riches when it comes to old cadavers, especially old female cadavers. What they prefer for their study are young cadavers. While I understand their scientific logic, I can't accommodate them unless they hurry up with that fountain of youth, and I am not absolutely certain I yearn for that. I find old age extraordinarily interesting.

My body is interesting, too. Naturally, all bodies are unique, but my body is exceptional. So much so that I was convinced it would provide valuable research material, and I offered this explanation to precede me to the medical school:

Beginning near the top, consider my ears. The ear is said to be the hardest organ to study because of its immediate changes after death. My ears are worth the bother not because of my slight hearing loss, which is about normal for my seventy-nine years, but because, from early childhood, I have had a wretched lack of balance. Specialists of the ear, where such problems normally reside, have not been able to diagnose the cause of the problem. There are probably children right now–maybe some of the very ones on my street–who fall down so much that they are hardly recognizable unless they had an egg-shaped bump on their foreheads, children who take twice as long as the rest of the kids to learn to skate or ride a bike, children who are the last chosen for all games and who freeze up at the thought of climbing a tree.

Delightful to dream that my cadaver, my ears, might help some of those needy youngsters get into good, normal, climbing and competing mischief and grow up able, as I am not, to pass a sobriety test when cold sober.

Then there are my eyes–very interesting, too, but possibly not to students of ophthalmology. Glaucoma was apparently a tendency inherited from my father; the myopia, astigmatism, and cataracts can probably be attributed to "nurture not nature," for my parents were convinced that good little girls should spend most of their time reading nice little books. Still, my eyes are somewhat interesting, for, after receiving a lens implant at the age of seventy-six, I acquired 20/20 vision. Though I still have sub-normal balance, I no longer get dizzy on mountain roads as I did in my myopic past.

On to the brain: at seventy-nine, my brain may be only mildly interesting since I seem (to me) to still have most of my marbles. But who knows? If, as I plan, you don't take delivery of my brain until I am ninety-eight or nine, it might have some scientific value, with or without marbles.

The really scientifically challenging part of my cadaver is my body. To help make the best possible use of this gift to your medical research, I must tell you of a number of pertinent facts about this body of mine.

You will hardly need to be told that my five-foot, two-inch skeleton (which is not sanforized, so it may be shrinking some) is truly heavy-boned for its height. A kind gift of nature (see ears) that destined me to take many, many falls from childhood on, some quite formidable falls, which would have cracked up most bones but spared mine. I've referred for years to these relatively unbreakable bones of mine as dinosaur bones, a term I found less reassuring when I learned that dinosaurs, like me, suffered from arthritis.

My bones do not now, and, I trust, never will, suffer from osteomyelitis.

Fierce with Reality

The reason for this is that I follow a firm antiosteomyelitis regimen: I chew on bones, eat allegedly calcium-rich food and take oyster shell tablets for starters, and then I get to the really important part of the program–I walk, walk, walk–up and down hills, stairs, through parks, and do some daily exercises to boot, all to keep my aging bones encased with firm flesh and muscle.

The penultimate feature of my carcass, which you will be negligent indeed if you do not examine carefully, and learn from, is that my body presents the image of being two half-bodies of different women joined by chance at the waist.

"If you were to cut off at the waist," my father-in-law told me a half-century ago, "your top half would weigh about fifteen pounds." Now, he was a rancher who had butchered a lot of cattle, sheep, and pigs, so he knew what he was talking about. At that time, I weighed about 118 pounds.

As you can imagine, when I reached puberty, my massive-boned thighs and legs caused me much woe, which my long neck, narrow shoulders, and small breasts helped not at all. The medics consulted blamed a congenital glandular imbalance for the problem and tried several costly and ineffective experimental medications.

Later, I concluded that the glands doing me in might be taking their revenge on me for my mother's idea that good little girls sat still and read. So I married an impoverished Arizona homesteader and spent my early adulthood riding horses, doing hard, physical labor, and getting into a more active lifestyle.

In explaining the fine points of my unusual cadaver, I must not do what my genteel southern science teacher did sixty odd years ago when she taught us, complete with charts and diagrams, all about our wonderful bodies–all, that is, except our genitalia.

Of course, unless your medical school is staffed by Fundamentalists who believe those legends of the Methusalahs and other very late bloomers, you will hardly expect to find a uterus in my venerable cadaver. You will see that it has been excised by a stupid and knife-happy surgeon early on. He did spare my ovaries, which enable me to receive and give considerable heterosexual pleasure. Your scientific interest might lead you to ask: at what age did this woman cease receiving and giving sexual

176

pleasure? I must answer that question as my mother did shortly before her premature death while still a sexagenarian: "When that time comes, I will let you know."

For a biographical note on San Francisco writer **Josephine Alexander**, see the last page of her essay, "A Sort of Death" on page 158.

Save It

Rosie saves old mustard jars; Edna Mae saves socks.
Floss and Dot save anything they think they'll ever use.
Sadie saves from habit, Lou for a rainy day,
Maria just can't bear to throw unbroken things away.
John collects malt whiskey although he drinks mostly beer,
Harry saves old 78s though he can hardly hear.
Will keeps concrete statues standing around the yard,
And Joe has never thrown away a single Christmas card.
With things they mean to use again, and things meant just for show,
The old folks cupboards are full up; display shelves overflow.
And still they hunt for bargains; they stash, tuck away, and store.
With nooks and crannies all jammed full, still they're collecting more.
Laverne buys yards of gold brocade because the price is low,
A pitcher and five porcelain kittens playing in row.
She tells me why she needs them, her eyes twinkling as she grins,
"When this life ends, whoever has the most stuff wins!"

Helen Kivnick

Helen Kivnick has set this poem to music. She founded and directs City Songs, a program for urban youth that integrates social work and music to promote health. Trained as a clinical psychologist, Kivnick has worked for nearly thirty years in practice, programming, research and teaching concerning healthy life-cycle development and intercultural relations. In *Vital Involvement in Old Age*, she collaborated with Erik Erikson and Joan M. Erikson. She is a professor of social work at the University of Minnesota.

Old Man Coyote and His Mother-in-Law
Brule Sioux

*According to tradition among the Plains tribes, a man may
not speak to his mother-in-law. He is also forbidden to look
at her, name her, or sit in the same place where she sits. The
character Coyote has many roles; one is troublemaker. In the
following story, he breaks the rules.*

Once when Coyote's wife was away, his mother-in-law did his cooking.
She was careful to cook with her back to her son-in-law. When she had
food ready for him, she put it behind her on the floor.

After a few days, a blizzard kept the two inside. Since Old Man Coyote
was used to being outdoors and moving around, he felt bored by his
confinement. He said, as if talking to the teepee flaps, "I wish I had someone
to talk to."

"I do, too," replied the mother-in-law.

So they passed the time sitting by the fire, telling stories, and talking
of many things. When Coyote tried to sing, he was hoarse. The sounds
irritated his mother-in-law. "I wish he would be quiet," she said.

"I'm a better singer on a full stomach," Coyote replied slyly. As they
were eating their supper, he said, "It would be better to sit side by side so
she doesn't have to pass the food behind her."

She agreed, and they ate their meal sitting side by side, with their feet
pointed towards the fire. Coyote then began to beat his drum and sing
again. Once again, the mother-in-law found this annoying. She said, "It's
getting cold in here. We need firewood. Why doesn't he get us some?"

After returning with firewood, Coyote and his mother-in-law talked
for a while longer and then, feeling sleepy, they prepared for bed. She set

out the buffalo hides for him to rest on, and then made up her own bed. They lay down. Then Coyote complained, "It is still cold in here."

His sleepy mother-in-law replied, "Just put more wood on the fire."

Even when the fire was big, Coyote still felt cold. "I'm used to having my wife beside me to keep me warm," he grumbled. "Why don't you come over here? You are my wife's mother, and you should be twice as warm as she is."

The mother-in-law was tired of hearing him complain, so she left her bed and got under his buffalo hide. As soon as he fell asleep and began to snore, she quietly moved out and put the largest log from the fire beside him. Then she went back to her own bed. When Old Man Coyote woke up in the morning, he saw how he had been kept warm all night. Speaking directly to the flaps of the teepee, he said, "I hope my wife gets home soon."

A longer version of this tale is included in *Plain Indian Mythology*, edited by Alice Marriot and Carol K. Rachlin. Thomas Cromwell, 1975.

The Autocrat of the Breakfast Table

excerpts

Oliver Wendell Holmes

Men often remind me of pears in their way of coming to maturity. Some ripen at twenty, like human Jargonelles, and must be made the most of, for their day is soon over. Some come into their perfect condition late, like the autumn kinds, and they last better than the summer fruit. And some, that, like the Winter-Nelis, have been hard and uninviting until the rest have had their season, get their glow and perfume long after the frost and snow have done their worst with the orchards. Beware of rash criticisms; the rough and stringent fruit you condemn may be an autumn or winter pear, and that which you picked up beneath the same bough in August may have been only its worm-eaten windfalls.

Old Age–I make it a rule never to force myself upon a person's recognition until I have known him at least *five years.*

Professor–Do you mean to say that you have known me so long as that?

Old Age–I do. I left my card on you longer ago than that, but I am afraid you never read it; yet I see you have it with you.

Professor–Where?

Old Age–There, between your eyebrows–three straight lines running up and down; all the probate courts know that token–"Old Age, his mark." Put your forefinger on the inner end of one eyebrow, and your middle finger on the inner end of the other eyebrow; now separate the fingers, and you will smooth out my sign-manual; that's the way you used to look before I left my card on you.

Professor—What message do people generally send back when you first call on them?

Old Age—*Not at home*. Then I leave a card and go. Next year I call; get the same answer; leave another card. So for five or six—sometimes ten years or more. At last, if they don't let me in, I break in through the front door or the windows.

~

The most encouraging things I find in the treatise, "De Senectute," are the stories of men who have found new occupations when growing old, or kept up their common pursuits in the extreme period of life. Cato learned Greek when he was old and speaks of wishing to learn the fiddle, or some such instrument (fidibus), after the example of Socrates. Solon learned something new, every day, in his old age, as he gloried to proclaim. Cyrus pointed out with pride and pleasure the trees he had planted with his own hand. (I remember a pillar on the Duke of Northumberland's estate at Alnwick, with an inscription in similar words, if not the same. That, like other country pleasures, never wears out. None is too rich, none too poor, none too young, none too old to enjoy it.) There is a New England story I have heard more to the point, however, than any of Cicero's. A young farmer was urged to set out some apple-trees. "No," said he, "they are too long growing, and I don't want to plant for other people." The young farmer's father was spoken to about it, but he, with better reason, alleged that apple-trees were slow and life was fleeting. At last someone mentioned it to the old grandfather of the young farmer. He had nothing else to do, so he stuck in some trees. He lived long enough to drink barrels of cider made from the apples that grew on those trees.

There is one other delicate point I wish to speak of with reference to old age. I refer to the use of dioptric media which correct the diminished refracting power of the humors of the eye—in other words, spectacles. I don't use them. All I ask is a large, fair type, a strong daylight or gas-light, and one yard of focal distance, and my eyes are as good as ever. But if *your* eyes fail, I can tell you something encouraging. There is now living in New York State an old gentleman who, perceiving his sight to fail, immediately took to exercising it on the finest print, and in this way fairly bullied Nature out of her foolish habit of taking liberties at five-and-forty, or thereabouts. And now this old gentleman performs the most extraordinary feats with his pen, showing that his eyes must be a pair of microscopes. I should be afraid to say to you how much he writes in the compass of a half-dime—whether the Psalms or the Gospels, or the Psalms *and* the Gospels, I won't be positive.

But now let me tell you this. If the time comes when you must lay down the fiddle and the bow because your fingers are too stiff, and drop the tenfoot sculls because your arms are too weak, and, after dallying awhile with eye-glasses, come at last to the undisguised reality of spectacles—if the time comes when that fire of life we spoke of has burned so low that where its flames reverberated there is only the sombre station of regret, and where its coals glowed, only the white ashes that cover the embers of memory—don't let your heart grow cold, and you may carry cheerfulness and love with you into the teens of your second century, if you can last so long.

Oliver Wendell Holmes, doctor and literary critic, was a native of Boston, Massachusetts. His best known work, *Autocrat of the Breakfast Table*, a collection of essays on a wide variety of topics, was published in 1858. The essays first appeared in *Atlantic Monthly*. His son, Oliver Wendell Holmes, Jr., became a Supreme Court justice.

Ageism

Nursery Rhyme

What are old women made of?
What are old women made of?
Bushes and thorns and old cow's horns
That's what old women are made of.

Victorian period, Gloucester

From Glamour Girl to Social Pariah

Marie Mitchell Olesen Urbanski

I am coming out of the closet. Ladies don't tell their age. I do not know the exact age of some of my friends. I feel like someone at her first Alcoholics Anonymous meeting confessing, "I am an alcoholic." "I am sixty-six years old." Why do I feel this way? Why do most women feel this way? At a birthday party, they say, "ninety-six years *young*." Am I evil to have lived so long? Yes, to be old is *bad*: to be young is *good*.

I can't count all the white lies and flattery I've heard about my acting/ looking younger than I am; nor all of the euphemisms for *old*, from *senior citizen* to *mature*, that exist. Then there are all the jokes about old women that have entered the collective (unconscious) minds from comedians such as Johnny Carson, as well as the literary allusions. Pound's comes to mind:

> "There died a myriad
> And of the best, among them
> For an old bitch gone in the teeth,
> For a botched civilization."

As an English professor, I know there is much literary misogyny, but from history the only old women I remember are the wicked witches burned at the stake. Whether consciously or subliminally, the message is imprinted that old women are outcasts, marginal members of society. I wonder then how it is possible for an old woman to have what therapists say one must have–healthy self-esteem.

There was a brief period when I welcomed birthdays, when I was delighted with more candles. I was the shy middle daughter, the one who was sloppy and seldom noticed unless I misbehaved. Then it happened—a dramatic transformation from repulsive green caterpillar to monarch butterfly. I wasn't a skinny, grubby kid anymore but a blue-eyed blonde with good legs and figure. I possessed the power to attract attention, to win favors and deference from males effortlessly, just by the way I looked.

In school, the road to success was popularity with boys. Academic achievement was frowned on for girls, as was excellence in sports. (How well I remember the collective media sigh of relief when sports great Babe Didrickson married George Zaharias.) My early dates began at fifteen. I cared little about the boys, but I did care about what my sisters and friends thought of me. "Peer pressure," it's called today. I went out on blind dates or other dates I managed to contrive with boys whose rating was acceptable to these peers. I am not sentimental about the bad old days, but this custom of numerous dates was not as negative as it might seem. Unlike today, no sexual intercourse was expected, just a kiss on the third date. It gave young people a chance to shop around before making a commitment. Flirtation could be fun, and, in time, I dated boys to whom I was attracted.

Hollywood does not get the school dances from the Swing Era right, for example in *The Way We Were*. They were the source of great anxiety for girls, even the most popular. In both college and high school, the dance was dominated by the stag line, composed of extra males. For young women, an invitation to the dance was not enough; they worried that they might be "stuck," that no one would cut in. When you did get a rush, you flew above the floor in euphoria, but, if you were stuck, you crawled in humiliation. I was unaware of a feminist analysis in those days, but what this system meant was that you needed masculine approval *en masse* at every dance. At school, I was like a Miss America contestant, always on parade, with a smile on my face, even for the drips whom I might need some night to rescue me on the dance floor. A dual-fragmented self—I was a glamour girl who projected sexuality to disguise my troubled feeling that the life of the spirit should be my real priority.

There was an elaborate set of rules in the dating ritual. An invitation took precedence over school work. If you refused, your excuse was always another date, not that you wanted to study, which would have been the ultimate insult to your caller. Dating was serious business in the Southwest, where I grew up, because unescorted young women did not go out at night alone, even to the movies.

My mother said it was a man's world, so it made sense that a woman's sense of self was determined by men. Didn't they control everything? Take the movies—recently, I saw a rerun of *Sunset Boulevard*, a film starring Gloria Swanson and William Holden about an aging actress with a young lover, a film I had seen when young. I remember being disgusted with the old woman with her young lover, and feeling the proper revulsion the audience was supposed to experience when the desperate woman clutched the man in an overtly sexual way. Of course, it had to end with a dead gigolo. Not surprisingly, though, my viewpoint had changed the second time around. Forty years later, the star did not look old; in fact, she was in good shape. Why shouldn't she have a young lover? Ironically enough–I kid you not–*Sunset Boulevard* was followed by *Gigi*, with an aging Maurice Chevalier and youthful Leslie Caron. What a difference a May/December romance made when the man was old, the woman young. Since Gigi's mother was a former courtesan, the whole thrust of the film was that the rich old man was doing the young girl a favor to marry her. Certainly the age difference did not matter when there was True Love.

Many a Hollywood film shaped our fantasies. My dilemma was that love ended in marriage in the films, and, like Sylvia Plath's heroine in *The Bell Jar*, I could not reconcile fantasy with the lives of my mother and the other housewives I observed. Although I kept falling in love, I kept postponing marriage. Men came too easily.

I can still see my mother sitting in front of the mirror lamenting her prematurely gray hair. When my friend Paul was killed during World War II, she said, "He will always be young." At that time, I thought this was no consolation. Now I understand. My father was an executive at an oil company. Standard Oil had a policy of not hiring secretaries over thirty–their only jobs open to women. The company also fired the secretaries if they got married. My kind father pretended he did not know his secretary had married because she needed the money, but he never questioned the policy. Older secretaries he called "old biddies" with a disgusted tone.

All the messages imprinted on my mind were that old women were revolting, as indeed they are still imprinted on the minds of the young today. So how does one cope with the erosion of self-esteem in a world controlled by men who only value young women?

Aging comes slowly. Each day we are a day older, but it is the birthdays that hurt, especially the decades, beginning as early as twenty. In addition to birthdays, you realize you are aging as people change in their response to you. You feel the same; and, at first, you think the same of yourself as you did of your youthful self, but your attitude changes as it begins to reflect the negative opinions of others.

As they grow older, all people have a series of choices to make as to the extent they will try to disguise their age. Gray hairs came early for me as they had for my mother. As with my first reluctant perm at thirteen, I acquiesced to society's norms and dyed my hair for twenty-five years. Probably the cosmetics ads have done more damage, and continue to do more damage to women's sense of self than any other opinion-shaper. Pond's Cold Cream's famous "Always a bridesmaid but never a bride" slogan is echoed today, as is Jergens Lotion's promise of "younger looking skin." It has been said that cosmetics sell "hope," but after having written copy for an advertising agency, I viewed commercials with skepticism. Most blatant today is Oil of Olay, with its message that to look old is unseemly, inspiring fear in the audience to pressure them to buy its products. Then there is the question of weight, with which all American females are obsessed. Who can eat a hot fudge sundae or mashed potatoes and gravy without feeling guilty? Also, aging brings diminished metabolism to consume calories, so a woman has to diet perpetually to keep in style or to "let herself go."

The trend that I most deplore is cosmetic surgery. It has accelerated in popularity so that face-lifts, fat removal, silicone breast enlargement—surgery on every part of the body are commonplace. They seem a tragic waste of surgical skill and a travesty of society's priorities. Recently, I saw Phyllis Diller on the talk-show circuit extolling her numerous operations. She used to be funny when she joked about her husband Fang, but now, what spirit has she to offer? We need fat, wrinkled comedians to defy male-defined superficial values for women rather than a woman who risked death and suffered under the knife repeatedly for a mask of taut skin. She could more profitably have used her money to assist aspiring showmen, as men traditionally have done for young women.

Another decision to make in the twilight zone of aging is the senior citizens or golden age discounts. They begin as early as fifty. For years, I did not take advantage of these varying discounts, as I preferred not to face reality. I have seen letters written in rage to the advice columnists by people who were falsely accused of being eligible for these discounts.

Another rite of passage into old age is hearing loss. As with an illness or other incapacity, it takes time to recognize the gradual erosion of hearing. At first, there is denial; you think people are not speaking clearly. My students were the catalyst for me. I was having trouble understanding some of the women, so I did go through hearing tests and purchased a hearing aid. With the acceleration of noise pollution and loud music popular today, they are going to be even more prevalent in the future. Still many people are unwilling to accept help from a hearing aid because deafness is linked to the stigma of aging.

The worst way people have of dealing with aged women is by calling you "young lady." They aren't malicious, but they know they can't call you "old lady." What we need is a polite means of address like the French "Madame." That would eliminate the doctor half your age calling you by your first name, while expecting you to call him "doctor."

And yet, I have found in all of my relationships with people that if I refuse to accept my pariah status, they usually respond in kind. Perhaps the old should join with Jesse Jackson in a ghetto school when he has the minority students shout after him, "I am somebody." When I meet a man women are pursuing, my first thought echoes my mother's, "I am not going to enter that fried-chicken derby. I've been married." Even that bitter echo of her frustrated brilliance no longer applies. It is just one of many sounds resonating from the stars.

When you are young, you have a very romantic view of death … perhaps you may die. Old people know they are going to die. Not unlike living in war time, I feel a greater intensity of living. Joy in a wild flower or a child or a cloud—in a moment. As with most of the aging, I fear disability and Alzheimer's disease more than death. Each day begins as a gift.

I want to work with a group like the Grey Panthers and boycott Oil of Olay and other products that blackmail and denigrate women. As in the Sixties when Black became beautiful, supplanting light skin and straightened hair (in style) as a guideline for beauty, we can change people's perception of advancing age to natural rather than unsightly. An aging face could be seen as an affirmation of life rather than as something shameful to be hidden, as menstruation once was, or cut away with the surgeon's knife.

I want old people to join my leap out of the closet. We live in the age of support groups in which we let all of our vulnerabilities hang out. Old people are not necessarily good or interesting. We are just people, as are the young. I remember listening to an advocate for the handicapped asking people to look beyond the wheelchair. He addressed his audience as the "not yet handicapped," to which I could add, "not yet old"–if you are lucky enough to live long. I look for the day when the old will be congratulated for being ninety-six years *old*, and when the young are not taught to dread old age.

I have been talking too much of exteriors, except when I spoke of my glamorous youth that disguised a tormented seeker. My outer shell is deteriorating, no doubt about it, but this is not necessarily true of the spirit. My elusive quest is less elusive. In the tradition of the Cherokee Indians I am connecting with the Grand Design of the universe. The path offers freedom from Illusion, a means to concentrate on my own psyche, less moved by the actions of others. With fewer options to distract me, I can devote more energy to the spiritual. My circular journey has taken me back to where I began as a grubby little kid. No longer arresting in appearance, I can still skin my knee as I did so many years ago and pick myself up when I fall.

Marie Mitchell Olesen Urbanski moved to Virginia after her retirement from the University of Maine and married Joseph Boyd Whittaker. After his death she moved to North Carolina, where she is writing her memoirs and promoting her second book on Margaret Fuller, *Margaret Fuller: Visionary of the New Age.*

Old in Spirit: A Gerontology Internship

Margaret Cruikshank

"Young in spirit? Why on earth should I want
to be young in spirit? I like being old in spirit
—my spirit is growing too."
—Sunlight

After finishing coursework for a gerontology master's degree at San Francisco State, I did an internship at Uptown, a large senior center where I organized an informal class called "All About Aging" and worked with the center's political action committee. Observing, attending programs and talking with seniors in the hallways and lounges taught me a great deal about aging. Work at a senior center differs from work in other settings because people disappear, they die, go into the hospital, or enter a nursing home.

I found the old men softer, kinder, more aware of feelings, more relaxed, more fun and less macho than their younger counterparts. I noticed that even the slightly-stooped men close to ninety carried with them an air of authority that goes with being male in our culture. But they seemed comfortable surrounded by strong old women in leadership roles.

The people I got to know at Uptown seemed relatively free from a need to conform to others' expectations of them, a trait that may be common to many of the healthy old. Several widows said that having given much to others all their lives, they were now loving the chance to please only themselves. "I've earned this right," a woman told me emphatically. Saying no brought a freedom they appreciated. Both women and men were free of a superficial politeness. Some barged into class late, got up out of their chairs to disagree with me, loudly, or to argue with each other, and walked out when they became bored. One day an old man in the back row snapped, "Why aren't more men here?" "Women tend to live longer than men," I replied mildly. "That's because women don't take care of their husbands," he roared back. I was startled by the fury on his face. It must be unsettling to be a man of eighty-five or older and find so few other survivors.

~

I was struck by the strength of the affectionate bonds uniting the core group in "All About Aging." They clearly felt solidarity with other old people. In a culture that devalues the old, they were dissenters. Some of their peers dissociate themselves from the old, for example by avoiding senior centers or programs geared specifically to people over sixty-five. At Uptown, being old was a strength, not a source of shame. The phrase "successful aging," a favorite of gerontologists, made a few of them smile, for they detected in it the prescriptions and expectations placed upon those whose situation is defined as a social problem.

Nevertheless, the members of Uptown senior center were honest about the dilemmas they faced. My graduate school gerontology classes looked at aging so positively that I was not prepared to confront the many demoralizing aspects of it about which I became aware at Uptown. The slow decline of one's physical power is infuriating, for example. Friends and spouses die, and funerals become depressingly frequent. Fear of confinement in a nursing home as frequently expressed by the seniors with whom I worked. The cost of living in San Francisco alarms them. They know one slip can put them in the hospital, perhaps for a long time. In many cases, their children live far away. The fear of becoming dependent–in any way–weighs on them. In other cultures, all the interconnections people have throughout life, necessary for their survival, sustain them in old age. Our fierce self-reliance and need for independence are not useful values to carry into old age. As we discussed this idea in class, I could see the seniors' dilemma: on the one hand, they wanted to be seen as independent because that was a source of pride; on the other, they knew they needed some kinds of help, at least occasionally. Even though they sometimes recited the miseries of aging with defiance and resignation, their situation seemed far less gloomy than that of the old characters depicted in literature. Thus it seemed that if the discipline of gerontology overemphasizes the positive aspects of aging, the literary images are unduly pessimistic.

~

The most valuable experience I had at Uptown was knowing Frieda Walter, an intense and high-spirited woman in her late eighties. As a young woman in Germany, working as a private secretary for doctors and lawyers, she spoke and wrote French, German, and English. As we became friends, I saw that she had mild dementia. Twenty-three of her relatives including a twin brother had been killed at Auschwitz. "I've cried so much in my life that I want to laugh now," Frieda told me. I admired her life force and her sweet, affectionate nature. When a worker at the center noticed that I liked to sit with Frieda, she growled, "You can talk to that one all day and never get from A to B." I was glad I had gotten a clear impression of Frieda's individuality before learning the category she had been assigned by the label "demented." I tried to focus on all the reasoning power "that one" had left rather than on her losses. Frieda told me, for example, that if she forgot what day it as, she called the operator. The creative twists and leaps of her conversation and her wonderful stories made me think that rational thought, as a sign of one's worth, is overrated. Sharing in Frieda's intuitive flashes was far more interesting that going from A to B. And, before long, the many repetitions in her speech stopped seeming like unfortunate lapses and instead took on a ritual quality. They meant something besides illness. Dementia is tragic because it severely limits one's ability to enter into the lives of others. But it is not a condition that robs one's life—or one's speech—of meaning. And each person who has dementia is unique.

At times, Frieda functioned rather well; at other times, she seemed a lost soul, when, for example, she would wander around the center clutching IRS forms and showing them to anyone who would listen. She knew her mind was not working right; sometimes she would point to her forehead and say, "*meschugge*" (crazy).

Often she told me that a wealthy man, who had loved her many years before in Germany, wanted to give her a large sum of money and came to the Uptown Center looking for her. I liked this story because of the man's wonderful name, Zelmar Zingman. Of course, the story seemed improbable, but I accepted its truth for Frieda and tried not to impose on it my sense of the demarcation between fantasy and reality. The emotional truth for her was that she had been loved in the past and was loved in the present. When she said of the Zelmar Zingman tale, "I'm glad I told you," she felt a connection to me that was real for both of us.

The first time Frieda told me this story, I was intrigued by the fact that, on that day, her talk was totally lucid except for the apparent fantasy about her old friend. I had thought dementia meant one crossed over some line into a shadow world and stayed there. Frieda moved back and forth between her private fantasy world and "normal" shared communication. An element of paranoia occasionally entered the story of Zelmar Zingman because Frieda believed his search for her was thwarted by the director of Uptown.

When we walked around Stowe Lake in Golden Gate Park, Frieda would interpret the low hum of distant traffic as words directed at her: "We love you, Frieda," is what she heard. Listening to her description of her devoted husband, Maxl, who had died only a few years before, I realized that Frieda had been deeply loved for many years, a more important fact about her than the fact that she occasionally heard voices, and I realized the futility and intrusiveness of my early attempts to explain the traffic noise to her as traffic noise. The Jewish holidays were very painful times for her because she missed Maxl then with special intensity. Some mornings, she said she wished she had died in her sleep. What can a friend say, confronted with the acute loneliness of someone who has outlived a beloved spouse? The story of Zelmar Zingman's search for her seemed an emotionally appropriate response to deep grief, a healing metaphor rather than a mere delusion.

Similarly, Frieda's stories of survival in Nazi Germany made me wonder about the power of the mind to recast real events in order to find some deeper truth than the literal truth. She told me that Maxl's non-Jewish family was determined to save her and showed much more courage than other families into which a Jewish person had married. Maxl's mother was a dressmaker who wore huge floor-length skirts. When the Nazis came looking for Frieda, her mother-in-law hastily stuck her under her skirts. Frieda was terrified lest she sneeze. She managed not to and was spared. The second story of her survival was simply that the family hid her in the garage, and the Nazis didn't think to look there. At first I wanted to know the *real* truth. Story two seemed more plausible, but story one was more satisfying because of its intimacy and display of quick wittedness. For Frieda, both were true. Having been loved in her long life, she had the power to make a new friend, even though she could not logically process much information from the friend.

On one occasion at the center, she inspired a protective love in me. As the members were celebrating Purim at lunch, Frieda got up and danced all around the huge dining room. She threw out her arms exuberantly. I feared she would be laughed at, but everyone accepted her spontaneous dancing. After lunch, she snatched a plant from the holiday table (plants were sold for $3.00 each after services). Frieda stuffed the plant into her tote bag, but the leaves were visible. Just then an official of the center grabbed another old woman who had taken a plant and yelled at her. I stood in front of Frieda to block his view, hurriedly led her out of the dining hall and found a plastic bag large enough to hide her plant.

She told me she liked me because I listened to her, and I told her I liked her because we laughed a lot. After my internship ended, I visited her in her apartment. Occasionally we strolled along Clement Street, where we had a favorite café. On these outings, I was struck by the power of her focus, when she gave attention to a flower, a sound, a baby in a stroller. Nothing else existed in that moment. Seeing the world through her eyes made me feel Zenlike not only because of her ability to focus but also because we walked very, very slowly, in a way I normally would not have had the opportunity to walk.

Because of Frieda's dementia, living alone was perilous. Her social worker and nearest relative, a cousin, wanted to move her out of her apartment. I thought she should stay. But I had no good answer to the social worker's question, "What if she leaves the burner on again and starts another fire and kills herself?" If only Frieda's welfare were involved, the risk might have been worthwhile, to preserve her autonomy, but others in her apartment building might have been harmed by her forgetfulness. Were the benefits of living on her own worth the risk? A tough call.

As I talked with the social worker and the cousin, I saw that our values were different. For them, Frieda's dementia was all-defining, not a trait or a handicap but an identity. They were appalled that she wore the same coat and dress every day and that her apartment was dirty and cluttered. Her safety mattered more to them than her autonomy. So they took her to a nursing home and asked her to sign a waiting list. She refused. This they took to be a sign of her dementia; I took it as a sign of her determination to hang onto her freedom. The cousin got conservatorship. Frieda was put into the home against her will. I believe she was institutionalized not because she had dementia but because her dementia caused extreme discomfort to her social worker and her cousin. In a sense, then, she was punished for their problem. Certainly they felt real concern for her and acted in a way most professionals would consider proper.

For me the most upsetting part of the abrupt move was that Frieda was put on a floor with Alzheimer patients and people with severe dementia; overnight her social world shrank immeasurably. Living on her own and walking daily to the Uptown Center, she came into contact with many people, a few of whom were demented. At the nursing home, she was cut off from everyone except those who could not talk to her. The first time I visited her, I saw in her eyes a look of extreme bewilderment as the people around her babbled on. One pounded our heads with an empty toilet paper roll; a second swore violently at us; a third took off all her clothes. I spoke with a social worker about transferring Frieda to another floor. The social worker was sure that the psychiatrist had made the correct diagnosis (the shrinks always asked the old, "Who is the President?" I don't know if Frieda passed that part of the test, but a friend's aged mother, when asked, snapped, "Reagan, that bastard"). Tragically, the placement of Frieda in the dementia ward, by people who hadn't the time or interest or skill to determine the real condition of her mental processes, resulted in her deterioration, so that a review of her "case" would justify the original placement. Her friends at Uptown know Frieda didn't belong in the dementia ward. They had seen her almost daily for many years; their assessment of her was far more accurate than that of the cousin, the social workers, the shrinks.

Frieda became very depressed, although occasionally I saw flashes of her old spirit when we strolled through the halls of the home and walked the grounds. Then she could have normal, friendly exchanges with the people she encountered, a few of who remember her from Uptown, where her fondness for dancing got her the nickname "the ballerina." As a free woman, Frieda took no medicine. In the institution, she was, of course, given drugs. Her ankles stayed badly swollen for months. She got dizzy. She fell recently and broke her wrist. Her depression, a natural reaction to losing her home and being placed in unfamiliar surroundings, was probably also caused by the drugs. Frieda was safer at home before she was taken away to make her safe. "I need someone who knows me well," she said to me one day. Sad words, because Frieda will never be known on Ward A, much less known well. Sad also because this "demented" woman is still capable of making as astute an assessment of her situation as any of us is likely to make.

Frieda can't leave the dementia ward. Patients are not told the special code that operates the elevator: 1, 1, 5, 7, 9. The other day she glanced at the white plastic band on her wrist, the kind hospitals use, and she said, "The state gives us these." She wears a different dress every day now, and her hair is trimmed and combed more frequently than before. Her small room is very neat. Musical programs at the home cheer her up somewhat, and she loves the Jewish services on Saturday. Frieda knows the prayers and hymns by heart. She remembers every word.

Sunlight (author of the epigraph) is a writer and artist living in Mendocino County, California.

Margaret Cruikshank taught English for many years at City College of San Francisco. She is currently a lecturer in women's studies at the University of Maine and the University of Southern Maine. Her book *Learning to be Old: gender, culture, and aging* was published in 2003.

from Quiet Fire: Memoirs of Older Gay Men
Interview with Jordan Lee

Keith Vacha

Years ago I had been puzzled why so many people wouldn't pay attention to me anymore. I kept thinking that there must be some monstrous defect in me. By then my weight was normal; I didn't have too bad a body though I had gray hair–I'd had it since I was thirty. At the same time, I had joined an all-male encounter group. I was the oldest member, a man in his late forties. The rest ranged from twenty-four to thirty-two.

One evening they spontaneously started discussing their sexual fantasies about one another. There were about twelve men in the group. As they went around the circle happily smiling at one another, getting closer and closer to me, I realized more and more that I was the eternal outsider. Everyone had fantasies about everyone else. No one had the slightest approximation of one about me. I realized that for many younger gays nothing is important about older men but their age. Many people liked me. Most of them valued my knowledge and experience. They didn't mean to make me unhappy. It was that they merely believed that an older gay man is sexually non-existent. They might have wished me to be happy, but always with someone else. My experience with that group drove home to me as perhaps nothing else could have the fact that I was an older man and what my status was as far as the gay world was concerned.

About eleven years ago, during Gay Pride Week, a seminar was held at Bethany Church. One workshop was about the problems of being older and gay. About six of us attended that workshop, and one woman said, "Pity we can't have a group to talk about these things." That led to a lot of discussions, and eventually we got a group together and found a place to meet.

My theory is that because gays didn't have a sense of group identity until recently, only since the late sixties, they didn't wake up to the fact that it was possible for them to grow older. It's part of the general American pattern about youth. In this country the two groups most fixated on being young forever are straight women and gay men. Lesbians are the most emancipated. As one lesbian explained to me, they had to free themselves from conventional notions about women being women and looking sixteen until they were eighty. There has been a lot of blocking out of the idea of growing older in gay circles. That is partially why there is a good deal of rejection of older men, especially within the city. A lot of people in the gay ghetto honestly believe that they will not live beyond thirty, if that long. And when they hit forty, that is going to be a world disaster. Many younger men won't patronize bars, baths, or other places where they think they'll encounter older men. Consequently, some places do their best to keep the older ones away. So we are part of a movement to try to rectify that imbalance. Many of the younger ones feel that older gays are slavering after their bodies. In reality, I, like most older men I know, prefer men near my own age. The basic life experiences are incommunicable; you have to have been through love and death and loss before you truly comprehend what they're like. I also agree with one man in his sixties who says, "I like sex, but I like it with someone who's read a book."

So far as I can see, older gay men have substantially the same problems as straight older ones, but with the added dimension of being gay. There's the worry of finances, a fixed income in inflationary times. Employment– how do you prove they don't hire you because you're older, if they don't say that's the reason, even if you know it is? Or that you are gay–an older man living with another and never married? Older people are not usually looked upon as a needed part of the community, gay or straight. I hope this will change. In G40+ [a support group for older gay men in San Francisco], we have changed our attitudes about becoming older. Being among our peers and seeing how many of us are leading full, successful lives is stimulating. We are enjoying our lives with gusto and are more at ease with ourselves than in adolescence. Most of the members lead fulfilling sex lives. And if you take care of yourself, your health can be good, too.

However, it's terrifying to think what it might be like to be in your eighties, incapacitated and in a straight convalescent home. You're possibly bedridden, more or less helpless. What will it be like to be looked after by persons perhaps kind enough but who don't understand? There are already older lesbians and gay men in such circumstances. We know they're there, but for the most part we have no way of contacting them. And how many doctors are generally aware of the problems of gay people? There are still many, many parts of this country where it's dangerous to reveal yourself, even to doctors. And if they don't know your special problems, what would be the good of it? Fear, too, is more deeply implanted in us than in younger persons. How do you possibly come out after forty years of hiding or leading a double life? It's gone on for so long you've forgotten any other mode of existence. There are a few groups for older gays in this country, only a handful. In many places, there are no gay organizations whatsoever.

There are special problems, too, about the loss of your partner of twenty or forty years. Unless the deceased partner has taken special legal steps, his family may possibly seize all his property, even though you and he have pooled your expenses all those years. Where do you go if you're bereaved? If you have a strong friendship network, they'll rally to you, but, otherwise, who or what is there?

Despite the possible grimness of all this, I would never again want to be even ten years younger. I'm now experiencing a degree of inner peace and self-acceptance and confidence I never knew before. I'm not altogether sure I'd like to be younger in the world in which younger people find themselves. Too, I'd say that most older gay men I know are happier than the younger ones. They seem more relaxed about who and what they are. They are worth knowing because they are survivors. And my experience of them, particularly the old ones in their seventies and eighties, is that they're pretty tough customers.

My advice is to become still, don't run around in circles. Just learn to relax. When your life alters, it seems to start inside of you. I have noticed how much better life is after I have done some form of meditation such as practicing tai 'chi. It forces me to develop a fresh direction. But I don't have all the answers. People are going to do what they want anyway. They want advice that echoes what they intend to do to begin with. They want sanction, not recommendation. That is something I do *not* anticipate will change with time.

The late **Keith Vacha** managed the Bethany Senior Center in the Mission District of San Francisco. His 1985 book *Quiet Fire: Memoirs of Older Gay Men*, edited by Cassie Damewood and published by Crossing Press, is a pioneering work.

The Fountain of Youth
Two Asian Versions

The Magical Spring

Tamae Nakahara

A long, long time ago lived an old couple who had a happy life helping each other. One rainy day, rain came inside their house. The old man told his wife, "I should fix the roof, but my body doesn't work as I wish it to. I feel sorry for you."

She answered, "Don't worry. I don't care."

Even though they had to make do and live without some things that they could no longer manage, their life passed peacefully in this way. They enjoyed each other's company and thought that they would live together happily even after their deaths.

However, an incredible thing happened to them. One day the old man climbed part way up a mountain to gather firewood. Remembering that his wife liked mushrooms very much, he decided to pick some for her. Then he climbed farther up on the mountain. But he got lost while he was picking mushrooms. "Where am I?" he said to himself. He felt so tired and thirsty. When he took a little rest, he heard the sound of running water. He hurried away in the direction from which the sound came through some trees. Finally, he found a small spring. "Water! Water!" he shouted and put his hands into the water. "How cold it is!" he drank slowly. "What sweet water this is!" He was surprised to feel completely refreshed. He drank again and felt his strength increasing. As he drank more water from the spring, he felt full of power.

On the surface of the water, his smiling face was reflected. But the face was not actually his. It was the face of a young man. This spring was special, one that returned people to youth. But the man didn't quite understand what had happened to him.

He returned home cheerfully and quickly. "Honey, I am home now," he called as he neared the house. "I'm sorry for being late. I got lost on the mountain."

"Who are you, young man?" said the old woman, thinking a stranger had entered her house.

"What are you saying? I am your husband."

"Huh? Whose husband are you?"

"Are you kidding me?"

"No! I am serious. Who are you?"

"Honey, it's me, your husband." He came closer.

"Your clothes are exactly the same as my husband's."

"Of course."

"Your voice is also the same."

"Of course."

"Oh! You have the same face he had in his youth."

The husband was surprised by her words. The face of his youth? He remembered the spring. Ever since he had drunk the water, he had felt something different about himself. Then he ran into the bathroom and filled the basin with water in order to look at his face.

"Who am I?" he asked.

"I don't know either," said his wife.

He looked again at his face reflected in the water. "It's me. It must be me. I became young. The spring must be a special one that returns people to their youths. How lucky!"

He jumped for joy as he told her about the spring. Then he brought a bottle from the kitchen. "I am going to draw water from the spring for you. You also have to become young."

"Not now," she replied. "Let's do it tomorrow."

"Can you wait until tomorrow?"

"Sure. Old people are more patient than young ones."

"All right. You are old, but only for today."

That night, even though the wife said that she could wait, she couldn't sleep due to her excitement. The next day, when the man woke up, his wife wasn't at home. He thought to himself that she had to have gone to find the spring. "She is going to surprise me," he thought. "All right. I will wait for her."

The old woman had left him at dawn. She walked to the spring the way her husband had told her. Toward evening, she had not yet come home, and the husband worried that she had gotten lost. He went to find her. He could run fast because he had become young.

When he approached the spring, he heard a baby crying. "A baby? Why?" The baby cried at the edge of the spring. The man looked carefully at the baby's clothes and discovered that they were those of his wife. Therefore, the baby must be his wife. "She must have drunk too much water," he said. Then he carried the baby home. Since that incredible thing happened to him, his life became very busy. He has had to take care of the child.

Tamae Nakahara of Japan was an exchange student at City College of San Francisco in 1989.

The Magic Pond

Tan Luong

This Vietnamese folktale is about an old woodcutter and his wife. They lived in the forest a short distance from the seashore. When they were first married, they were very happy, but, later, after their three sons were born, they grew apart. By the time the boys had become young men, the couple could best be described as miserable. The boys worked away from home from early morning until late at night. They had become fishermen and had little in common with their father. They always showed great respect for him, however, even though they had taken up fishing and not woodcutting as their professions.

Although the woodcutter and his wife were unhappy together, they felt great love for their children, and so, when a great storm came and the boys were lost at sea, the terrible news was all the harder to take. They felt overwhelming grief. Strangely, it was that grief that brought them together again. As the years passed, they became closer and closer, and, as their love grew, the pain of the past was softened. All their neighbors commented on their great love for each other.

Their bodies aged with the passing years. Their hair grayed; their skin wrinkled; they walked more slowly than before. The old man wondered why youth had passed them by, why they were such old people now. As he was tired, he sat down on the log he was cutting. He unpacked the afternoon meal that his wife had prepared for him. He ate quietly, thinking of what might have been. Since the day was hot, he moved to a place with more shade after he finished eating and quickly fell asleep.

He woke some time later, wondering about the dream he had just had. In the dream, an angel had listened to his story and felt compassion for him. The angel told him of a way he could live part of his life over again. The angel said that, because he was a good man, he would tell him of a secret pond, much deeper in the forest. If he drank a handful of water, he could be young again. He need only follow the blue bird to find the pond. "But that was a dream," the old man told himself. "There are no magic ponds and no blue birds in this forest. I'm getting too old to have my mind play tricks on me." He had lived his whole life in the forest and had never seen a blue bird. He went home and told his wife about the dream. She replied in a quiet voice, "Old man, you must be losing your mind. Don't talk of such foolish things in the village, or they will think you're crazy."

Several weeks came and went, and the old man forgot about the dream. One day while he worked, he was shocked by the sight of a beautiful bird, blue as the sky. He started to chase the bird. "I must be dreaming again," he thought, because, as he ran, he felt full of energy. After a few minutes, he came to a clearing, and there beyond the mist was a small quiet pond. He could not believe that he was awake, but, recalling what the angel had said, he scooped up a handful of water and drank it. All at once, he felt refreshed and very happy. When he looked at his reflection in the pond, he saw himself as he had looked at twenty.

The woodcutter ran all the way home to tell his wife of the miracle and burst through the door of his house. His terrified wife pleaded with him not to hurt her as she was an old woman who had nothing of value. He tried to convince her of his identity. It took much talking, but, after some time, she started to see in this man the image of her husband in his youth. He told her the story.

Early the next morning, the wife went into the forest to find the pond herself. At last, she found it, drank a handful of water and became young. She was so happy and excited. Now they were both young, and they had a chance to live their lives over again. But, if one handful of water could make her young, perhaps another drink would make her beautiful. She drank but too much. Instead of becoming beautiful, she became even younger, turning into a baby.

Meanwhile, her husband worried when she didn't come home and began searching the forest for her. He found the small baby. Knowing that it was his wife, he picked her up and carried her home in grief. He had lost her. Then he knew it was wrong of him to want to live his life over. He knew he was better off being old and having the love of his wife than being young and alone. Their love had resulted from their life together. It would not be the same now. The next morning, he took the baby to the temple to pray. He fed it and went to bed. Morning took a long time coming. When he opened his eyes, his back hurt, his feet hurt, and he felt tired. Then, suddenly, he heard a loud crash. He jumped to his feet to see what was wrong and saw his wife as she had looked two days before. Her hair was gray, her skin wrinkled. She had changed back! Again the husband thought he was dreaming. As he lifted his hand to wipe his eyes, he realized that his hand was wrinkled, too. He gave thanks to the angel for restoring them.

Tan Luong studied English at City College of San Francisco.

Reflections

Fierce with Reality

Zen Poems

Translated by Lucien Syryk

For eighty years I've talked of east and west;
What nonsense. What's long/short? big/small?
There's no need of the gray old man, I'm one
With all of you, in everything. Once through
The emptiness of all, who's coming? Who going?
                    —Kiyo

Light dies in the eyes, hearing
Fades. Once back to the Source,
There's no special meaning—
Today, tomorrow.
                    —Ktsuzan

I've crossed the sea after Truth,
Knowledge, that snare, must be defied.
Here and there, I've worn out heaps of sandals.
Now–moonlight water in the clear abyss.
                    —Kakua

An interview with **Lucien Syryk** appears in the July 1995 issue of *Poets and Writers*. He is the subject of a book by Susan Porterfield of Rockford College.

The Five Remembrances

I am of the nature to grow old.
There is no way to escape growing old.

I am of the nature to have ill-health.
There is no way to escape having ill-health.

I am of the nature to die.
There is no way to escape death.

All that is dear to me and everyone I love
are of the nature to change.

There is no way to escape being separated from them.
My actions are my only true belongings.

I cannot escape the consequences of my actions.
My actions are the ground on which I stand.

The Buddha

Buddha. Siddhartha Guatama, the Buddha ("the one who is awake"), born in the 6th century B.C. in what is today Nepal, began life as a wealthy prince. After encountering suffering, he adopted an ascetic, wandering life for several years. He attained enlightenment after sitting for many days under a bodhi tree. Buddha offered himself as a teacher rather than as a god.

On Gray Hair and Oppressed Brains
Ann E. Gerike

Gray hair is universally viewed as an indication of advancing age, though the age at which hair begins to gray varies widely among individuals. Changes in hair color begin sooner than most people realize. A study of Australian blood donors in 1965, for example, revealed that, by the time they were twenty-five, twenty-two to twenty-nine percent of the women had some obvious graying. The age at which people begin to gray seems to be genetically determined, as are the graying patterns.

Much of the gray effect is produced by the mixture of light and dark hairs, though as dark hair loses its color, it is genuinely gray for a time. Blond hair, of course, "grays" much less noticeably than darker hair. The proportions of white to dark hair has to be well over fifty percent before it begins to show decisively.

Little research has been done on the graying of hair, so much of what is known about it is assumption and guesswork but the basic process appears to be the following:

> Each of the 100,000 hairs on the head is controlled by a hair bulb below the follicle at the deepest part of the root system. It is through the hair bulb that a variety of complex substances are channeled, creating each hair, mainly composed of a biochemical substance called keratin.
>
> In the hair roots and in the epidermis, millions of protein-producing pigment cells, called melanocytes, produce chemicals that determine the coloring of hair and skin… The melanocytes, in turn, are responsible for chemistry that colors the hair that takes shape in the follicle and grows long enough, eventually, to be seen…

Melanin, the pigmentation chemical, has two components. The two basic colors predispose a hair to be dark or light or a shade between, depending on the proportion of each pigment that is genetically introduced into the hair-making process. Coloration is influenced by racial and ethnic factors, but virtually no research has been done on the existence of such influences in graying…

The color chemistry changes with age so that even a person who has no gray may find his or her natural hair coloring changing with advancing age. Many people experience a darkening in their coloring—directly attributable to the maturing function of the melanocytes and the varying production of melanin.

With time… the melanocytes weaken, and their pigment-producing chemistry begins to shut down. It is a gradual process, and, for the period that the melanocyte is still functioning at reduced capacity, the bulb may produce a hair that is gray, or incompletely colored. In time, though, the melanocyte stops working, and the hair bulb produces white hair. The process can also be influenced by a variety of diseases that prematurely—and sometimes reversibly—reduce enzyme chemistry and interfere with pigment cells. In the vast majority of cases, age and the natural evolution of melanocytes—culminating in their cessation of function —cause graying.

However interesting that explanation may be as a description of biological process, the graying of hair is interesting primarily for sociological, not biological reasons. For, of course, millions of women, and increasing numbers of men, color their hair because of the negative myths and stereotypes about aging that form the basis of ageism in our society. These negative attitudes are implicit in our language: "old" is assumed to connote incompetence, misery, lethargy, unattractiveness, asexuality, and poor health, while "young" is used to imply competence, happiness, vitality, attractiveness, sexuality, and good health. People are told they're "as young" (or "only as old" as they feel, and they are admonished to "keep themselves young." When they are ill, they are said to have aged; when they recover, they're told they look younger.

The coloring of gray hair disguises the physical feature associated with aging that is most obvious and most easily changed. Such hair dyeing, in our youth-oriented culture, represents the attempt of aging people to "pass" as members of a group with greater power, privilege, and prestige than the group to which they in truth belong. In that, it is similar to the widespread use of skin lighteners by many blacks in the time preceding the Civil Rights movement.

In a patriarchal society, the power and privilege of women reside in their utility to men. They must be able and willing to bear children and be willing to remain in a subservient position. In such a society, women beyond menopause are useless; they obviously cannot bear children. They may also be dangerous: with the growing assertiveness that often comes to women as they age, many are unwilling to remain subservient.

If a women's choices are to be either useless or dangerous as she ages, it is perhaps no wonder many women prefer to use hair color as a means of concealing—or at least underplaying—their age.

Since traditional male socialization does not encourage men to acknowledge their "weaker" feelings, women have often taken on the role of caring for men's emotional as well as their physical needs. The fact that women expend far more time, money, and effort in attempts to retain a youthful appearance than do men may well represent an aspect of such emotional caretaking. By providing men their own age (usually their husbands, but sometimes their lovers) with a false-faced mirror of youth, they may be attempting to protect such men from the emotional reality of aging and eventual death. In the film *Moonstruck*, a white-haired Olympia Dukakis asks, "Why do men chase women?" and answers herself: "Because they fear death." I once heard a man say to his gray-haired wife, without rancor: "I only feel old when I look at you."

At the same time, of course. The woman may be protecting herself, or at least attempting to do so. A gray-haired or white-haired woman is often seen as motherly, and sexual attraction to the mother is taboo.

The assumption that women are no longer sexual beings when they have passed their childbearing years is clearly an aspect of patriarchy. The desexualizing effect of gray hair is well-illustrated by the experience of a friend of mine, who had grayed in her late teens and had never colored her hair. When she was in her late thirties, she dyed her hair black, on a dare. The next day, when se went to the gym she had been attending for some time, she suddenly materialized for men who had not previously noticed her.

Such magical invisibility is not only sexual; it is pervasive, similar to that noted long ago for blacks by Ralph Ellison in *Invisible Man* (1952) and James Baldwin in *Nobody Knows My Name* (1961). The title of Barbara Macdonald's powerful treatise on ageism, *Look Me in the Eye* (1983), addresses the fact that, in most social circumstances, women as well as men seldom make eye contact with the old, whom they simply do not see. If old women are not ignored, they are often subjected to a condescending headpatting kindliness that suggests that its recipient is unintelligent, uneducated, and incompetent. That women should want to avoid such treatment as far as possible is understandable, and they may be able to avoid it for a time by coloring their gray hair.

Sexism in combination with ageism also causes women problems in the job market as they age. Many women dye their hair because they fear, perhaps with good reason, that they might lose their jobs, or find it difficult to obtain jobs, if their gray hair were visible. In many professional circles, gray hair on women is considered unprofessional. Office workers in particular are often chosen for youthful physical appearance.

Despite the advances of feminism, ageist standards of appearance were seldom challenged before the last few years, probably because most women in the latest wave of the movement could, until relatively recently, have considered themselves young. Now that the Baby Boom generation is entering middle age, however, that situation is beginning to change. But I am not aware of any overt attempts by feminists to raise consciousness specifically on the issue of gray hair. Elissa Melamed, in her book on ageism and its effects, *Mirror, Mirror: The Terror of Not Being Young* (1983), talks at length about cosmetic surgery and skin treatment and their ageist implications, but dismisses hair dyeing with one sentence: "Covering gray is so simple and commonplace that there is no longer much emotional charge about it."

Internalized ageism, an acceptance of the status quo, is no doubt one reason why little has been written about gray hair; earlier, male domination was also considered "simple and commonplace." Another reason may be a reluctance to "blame the victim." Women clearly are the victims of ageism, and older women may be struggling to do their best in a world where they are disproportionately the victims of poverty. While it might theoretically be better for them to challenge ageism, they may be fighting other battles that consume most of their energy.

Increasingly, however, gray hair can be an advantage for a woman who is already in a position of authority. A friend of mine, for example, a medical resident, found her students much easier to manage when she let her naturally gray hair appear. I myself suspect that my almost-white hair gives me "clout," even though I entered my profession, clinical psychology, late in life. One might assume that having gray or white hair would be an advantage for those working with an older population, as I do; but the majority of older women I know who work with the elderly dye their hair, perhaps out of fear of being identified with their clients.

Ultimately, the coloring of gray hair by women serves to endorse and to perpetuate both ageism and sexism. The world is full of gray and white-haired women who are living testimony to the advantages of age for women, but the power of their testimony is greatly muted by their dyed hair.

As women increasingly accept the reality that they have value in themselves, beyond their youth and serviceability to men, they will naturally be less likely to attempt to hide the normal effects of their age. Just as women have produced a less sexist world, so they can challenge ageism to produce a world in which women do not feel compelled to hide their age with hair dyes, face lifts, and other expensive stratagems.

The advantages of leaving gray hair untouched are many. It saves a considerable amount of both time and money. The natural affinity of hair and skin color is preserved. Skin tone also naturally changes with age, and women who color their hair usually have to expend considerable time and effort to make their faces match their hair. Unfortunately, the combination of old face and young hair is often discordant.

Hair may gray in interesting patterns, which are lost when the gray hair is colored. Women who allow their hair its natural changes also often find themselves able to wear colors that did not suit them in their younger-haired days. And they can preserve both their hair and their health: the use of hair dyes can contribute to hair loss, especially when combined with other harsh hair treatments,[3] and petroleum based dyes, usually in dark shades, cause cancer in laboratory animals and may pose a danger to users.[4]

The greatest advantage, however, is that a woman who allows her hair to gray naturally is accepting herself for who she is. She is also, in effect, challenging the ageism of a society that tells her she should be ashamed of her age and should make every effort to disguise it. Just as blacks took a physical feature associated with their blackness—naturally kinky hair— and flaunted the Afro, challenging the limited white standards of physical attractiveness, so aging women can flaunt their graying and white hair, challenging the blinkered standards of an ageist society.

Ann Gerike, a clinical psychologist and gerontologist, spent many years as an activist on women's aging issues. She now lives a relatively quiet life on Whidbey Island, where she is studying and writing poetry and short fiction. Her 1997 book *Aging is not a Four-Letter Word* sold over 9,000 copies

Notes

1. A. Parchini, "Scientists Still Haven't Gotten to the Roots of Gray Hair," *Minneapolis Star Tribune,* reprinted from *Los Angeles Times,* October 14, 1987. All factual information about hair presented here is from this article.
2. Ibid.
3. "Winning the Battle Against Hair Loss," *Harpers Bazaar,* August 1984.
4. P.B. Doress and D.L. Siegal, *Ourselves, Growing Older: Women Aging with Knowledge and Power,* New York. Simon and Schuster, Inc., 1987.

References

Baldwin, J. (1961). *Nobody Knows My Name: More Notes on a Native Son.* New York: Dial Press.

Doress, P.B. and Siegal, D.L. (1987). *Ourselves, Growing Older: Women Aging with Knowledge and Power,* New York: Simon and Schuster.

Ellison, R. (1952). *Invisible Man.* New York: Random House.

Macdonald, B. with C. Rich (1983). *Look Me in the Eye: Old Women, Aging and Ageism.* San Francisco: Spinsters Ink.

Melamed, E. (1983). *Mirror, Mirror: The Terror of Not Being Young.* New York: Simon & Schuster.

Parchini, A. (1987, October 14). "Scientists Still Haven't Gotten to the Root of Gray Hair." *Minneapolis Star Tribune,* reprinted from *Los Angeles Times.*

"Winning the Battle Against Hair Loss." (1984, August). *Harpers Bazaar.*

An Artist's Notes on Aging and Death
Vera Klement

When we talk about aging, another word keeps asserting itself. The other word, the word underneath the word aging, is death. To speak of death is to address the absolute center of human existence. Heidegger saw the human as a being-toward-death. A being that must be able to integrate death as part of life. Not as an accident that ends life, that occurs at the end of a life, but rather that of a being that places itself in the ending. End, not so much as a ceasing but rather as a fulfillment. Ending as completing.

Unfortunately, we don't have the tools for creating this mental construct. It is something an entire society has to have as part of its language. As individuals, we put off thinking about our own death. Not yet … later … when it becomes necessary, inevitable. When we are reduced to illness, to weakness.

Tolstoy gave us the most powerful vision of this in *The Death of Ivan Ilyich*. The suffering and dying Ivan Ilyich has no structure, no language available to him in which to experience the death he had in no way anticipated. The people around him, family, doctors, are evasive; they lie to him or avoid him because they don't know how to speak, how to acknowledge his dying. It is to him an experience of utter humiliation and abandonment. In the process of dying, he becomes socially unacceptable. An outcast. His death is seen, in the end, as an irritating interruption of a card game.

We have, in our culture, an unspoken agreement not to speak about our own death. Mention of it is withheld lest we appear tactless, self-indulgent, neurotic, morbid, or even cowardly. There is no precise language to name death, to accept death and our dead. Without such a language, we cannot integrate it. Integration requires metaphor and ritual. When, as a group, we are confronted with an image of dread, the group mind clangs shut. But it can be touched with the prick of a rose, with an image once removed. It is through the symbolic, the metaphors and rituals, that a group is able to integrate its fate collectively and individually.

When I was young, there were still a few vestiges that symbolized death and mourning. A person's grief was expressed publicly by wearing black. Now we neutralize death, make up the corpse to look still alive, and go on, business as usual.

Several years ago in Leningrad, now St. Petersburg, I visited the Lavra Cemetery, a popular excursion place. Large numbers came from all over the country to walk among the tombs of Russia's great: Moussorgsky, Tchaikovsky, Dostoevsky. The dead and their works assumed a presence in that context. They belonged to the crowd. In another park, near Moscow University, numbers of young couples, just married, the brides in white gowns, carrying flowers, stopped to lay the flowers at the tomb of the fallen soldiers of World War II. Their marriages were witnessed and sanctified by the dead. Our belief in science and the rational doesn't permit the dead to play a role for the living. Death as a thread woven into the social tapestry has vanished.

This is not to say that we lack images of death around us. Quite the contrary. Images of murder, war, famine, the catastrophe of AIDS, and every kind of human misery inundate us. Desensitize us. But those who die are others; they are not ourselves. They are there; they are not here. These images function to absolve and spare us. For the death of others, we have compassion; we group and categorize, sentimentalize and aestheticize it into TV dramas. Death becomes kitsch. This does not work when we become the sole actor.

In the nineteenth century, a romantic nihilism replaced the belief in individual immortality with the ideal of an immortal world, its art and its artifacts as its scripture. But by the twentieth century, after Auschwitz, after Hiroshima, even this pessimistic ideal became too hopeful. Hans Morgenthauc wrote, in the sixties, that the Cold War removed that slender consolation irrevocably. The Cold War opened up the possibility of total annihilation. With that an awareness took hold of the imagination that not only our bodies could be destroyed, but everything, everything we had thought to leave behind could vanish. The world as enduring place, our civilization constituting our continuity, that trace that was to contain our immortality was now threatened. A barbaric void opened up. Facing nothingness is repellent, indeed impossible. There is no language, no image, for nothing. The only possible response is denial. Denial embraces its opposite. The opposite of annihilation is life. And so we celebrate life by idolizing its representation, youth. Youth symbolizes the eternal present. In this belief system, youth, health, and beauty form a trinity that is the good and the true. Its church is the health club. If youth symbolizes life, then it is the aging who symbolize death. They are horrible reminders. They must strive to conceal their condition. We have developed many sophisticated methods of disguising the symptoms. To look one's age is socially incorrect. A woman suffers much more within this agenda than does a man. No longer a potential childbearer, she is also no longer a sex object and ceases to have any value. It is difficult for her to be a voice that is heard.

The denial of aging extends itself to the product of aging: the accumulation of knowledge, the experience of a particular time lived. But we insist that only the latest has value. We update. This places us in the present. The order of our time in the Now. And it is the new that maintains the Now. *The Tradition of the New*, as Harold Rosenberg so aptly called it.

I think there is a direct relationship between the denial of death and the kind of culture we produce. Popular music, amplified to the highest decibel, blinking intense light patterns, pulsing pornography are efforts to drown in the eternal present. The ubiquitous screen miniaturizes us into undifferentiated surfaces even as it engulfs us into its enlarged space. Fashion, the rapid changes of style in art, clothing, or food, although the product of an economy, has the same function. Dealers and collectors are ever on the lookout for the new, young artist with a vision that is relevant to the moment. In the fast turnover, in the production and reproduction of obsolescent objects, we confirm ourselves as expendable objects, replaceable by new, younger ones. We are obsolescent like the objects we produce.

This notion of seasonal new discoveries has a disastrous effect on the process of artistic development. Making art is hard. It requires a life-time. But it is assumed that talent is born, like Minerva, fully formed. An artist's gradual ripening, deepening, evolving, and finally enduring are hardly to be tolerated by a system with an insatiable desire for the new. The imperatives of marketing and the psychological drive to a constant present conspire to make a cumulative culture an impossibility, one in which the best of each moment would be accumulated, added on, gathered, so that change could become a dialogue between past and present. In this country, we tear wonderful old buildings down to make room for new faceless ones.

The attitudes of denial definitely have had an impact on the teaching of art. We no longer teach a body of knowledge, a visual language as exemplified in the works of previous masters. We do not teach the past. We teach the present. The force of the denial of death translates itself as the denial of a reverence for the dead, the past masters, and their works.

It is tragic that aging is not seen as it ought to be, the realization of an entire person. Age, Jung said, is the realization of the innate idiosyncrasy of a living being.

Anthony Storr, the British psychiatrist, describing the stages of a creative personality, says that, in the third and last stage, the artist becomes less concerned with the rhetoric of communication and is looking rather into the depths of her own psyche. This is accompanied by a greater desire to be alone. In solitude—to be differentiated from isolation—there is room for an expansion of the self, an intuition of connections. This stage can be a remarkable time for an artist's work. Techniques, having long ago been internalized, are mute and express themselves as imagination.

In conjunction with solitude, there is a longing for silence, a silence increasingly sought by the aging as they approach death, a silence necessary for reflection, for realization. Memory stirs in silence.

Silence: a metaphor for death.

The maximal condition for the creative act is silence. Can we not say then that in silence a space opens up in which the making of art that is a gift becomes possible? And that act occurs in the silent space that holds the full awareness of one's death, one's ending/completion. It is in the making of this gift that life, the partner of death, is celebrated.

Vera Klement was born in 1929 in the Free City of Danzig (now Gdansk, Poland). A painter who has exhibited internationally, she is a Guggenheim Fellow and the recipient of an NEA grant. She was Professor of Art at the University of Chicago for twenty-five years until her retirement in 1995.

Toward More Human Meanings of Aging
Ideals and Images from Philosophy

Geri Berg and Sally Gadow

Note: the original, longer version of this essay included reproductions
of paintings and was titled, "Toward More Human Meanings of Aging:
Ideals and Images from Philosophy and Art."—Ed.

Aging has always been a problematic experience. We may believe, at
times, that our century is unique in viewing aging as problematic, but the
same ambiguity that surrounds aging now was known to our predecessors:
"When death approaches...old age is no burden." The tacit implication
is that old age is indeed a burden, made lighter only by contemplation of
some alternative. To the young, aging is no better than death, while to
the old, aging may be life itself, as precious and irreplaceable as youth to
the young.

This ambiguity permeates all of our thinking about aging. We are not
sure whether it is a phase of living that is both healthy and normal, or
unhealthy but still normal, or whether it is unhealthy and abnormal. Is it
a stage of life or simply the earliest stage of dying? Is being old worth one's
whole life to attain? Shall we revere it, prevent it or cure it? Are we to
anticipate growing old with hope, dread, or indifference?

We often approach a difficult problem by trying to understand two
things about it. We ask: (1) What is it? How shall we define it? (2)
What is its value? Usually, we assume that modern science should answer
the first, the humanities the second (science being value-free and the
humanities value-oriented). But, in fact, because aging is a profoundly

human experience and not a purely natural phenomenon, like trees losing their leaves, its definition and its value are inseparable. We cannot answer the questions of what value and significance it has for us.

Indeed, the sciences themselves reflect this inseparability. In their account of the "facts" about aging, the physiological, psychological and socioeconomic sciences offer us their definitions. The physical sciences suggest that aging is thus far an irreversible, physiological deterioration, a disorganization and disintegration characterized by predictable deleterious changes from total body movement to the level of cells and molecules. The behavioral sciences describe aging as a set of processes resulting in failing mentation, confusion, memory loss, and disorientation. Furthermore, the social sciences inform us that aging is characterized by decreased economic productivity; by social isolation due to non-employment, dying peers, and the exclusively nuclear family; and often, by total dependence upon others. These are the so-called "facts" about aging and value-free as they are supposed to be, they offer us not a neutral view but an altogether negative one. This "definition" presents an interpretation that not only implies what aging is, but also what *significance* it has, and that significance is negative. Medical science, in turn, expresses and applies this negative valuation by treating aging as a disease. All that is missing from the clinical model is a clear cause and a cure (and theoretically both can still be discovered).

What this indicates to anyone not already persuaded, is that we cannot define a human experience with facts alone. We invariably interpret and evaluate the facts in some way. Cellular changes, for example, are not described simply as specific chemical and structural transformations but as "deterioration." It is thus more honest and useful to acknowledge that we are never talking about the facts as distinct from the value of aging, but are always formulating a view of the two together. In other words, we are not, even in science, expressing a final *definition* of aging but rather some tentative meanings of aging.

If one such meaning is that which science and medicine offer, what reason is there to seek further meanings from the humanities? The reason is this: the humanities are concerned not only with understanding as fully as possible the depth and scope of human experience—this, they share with the sciences —but, beyond this, they are concerned with creating or uncovering more human meanings for our experience. Thus the humanities are ultimately engaged in formulating ideals. By "ideal" or "more human meaning" is meant a way of understanding an experience that enhances the value of the experience for the individual, and at the same time preserves the element of freedom in human existence by opening a door to new possibilities. It might be phrased this way: wherever a locked door presents itself in our experience, a closure that means "here is the limiting concept, feeling, insight, beyond which there is no further understanding of this phenomenon," there, the task of the humanities is to provide a key, either one long forgotten in history or one newly created for just that door.

The negative meaning of aging is such a door. Insofar as it limits our understanding of aging to the notion of decline, without leaving open the possibility of alternatives, that meaning is not as human as we would wish. It is not yet ideal. Perhaps it is one facet of a larger understanding, but, in itself, sheer decline or disintegration is not a sufficiently human meaning of aging.

Our intention is to explore some meanings that are more expressive of the fact that aging is a human experience—not simply a physiological-psychosociocultural-economic experience. And, in effect, since we are concerned here with finding meanings alternative to the negative interpretation from science, we are concerned with uncovering or generating positive meanings.

By positive, however, is not meant aging-with-a-happy-ending, or aging that is itself a happy ending. For example, one popular candidate for a positive meaning of aging is the view that one's later years can be rendered as nearly "normal" as possible. Aging is a time in which, barring a few extra maladies, nothing changes. One continues to work, to be active, independent, maintaining the same scope and intensity of social and professional involvement. This positive value of aging is more accurately a neutralization of the negative value, achieved by means of omitting, ignoring, or bypassing aging. It amounts to a false positive, because it assumes that the only way of making aging human is to make it as nearly like youth or mid-life as possible.

From these two views—the negative and the false positive—we can learn something about what a genuinely positive meaning of aging would be. these views are limiting because the one hopelessly overvalues, the other undervalues, the realities of aging: that the body moves slowly, that the senses alter, that some structures grow rigid while others become flaccid, that the skin folds back upon itself, that the memory winds around and restructures itself, that some capacities disappear, and that somewhere dying begins. For the negative view, these spell the doom of aging (or the disease called aging). For the stay-young view, they are excluded from aging.

In searching for more human meanings, then, we can begin by neither devaluing nor ignoring the reality of these processes but only by accepting them as ciphers, symbols, keys to possible meanings. The meanings that we will propose here are one attempt to interpret these ciphers as possible answers to the question that the humanities alone can answer: Where does aging fit in an ideal scheme of things? What is the value of aging in an ideal human existence?

Processes of Aging as Symbols of Meaning

Slowing down—opening time. The slowing process in aging is one of its most dominant symbols or, in clinical terms "symptoms." How can that phenomenon be understood in such a way that it illuminates in more human terms the experience of aging?

It may be that aging is the part of our lives in which our being slows on all levels in order to experience situations and persons with more attentiveness and care than is possible when a youthful, fast-paced metabolism and an energetic, vigorous body inspire us to cover great distances at high speed, to finish quickly with one experience in order to hasten on to the next. It may be that with age we realize time has the dimension of depth as well as duration. For most of us, these two dimensions seem to be an either/or, and it is only when the aspect of duration is seen not to be endless that we fully recognize the aspect of depth or density of time. We slow ourselves then to explore experiences, not in their linear pattern of succeeding one another, but in their possibility of opening for us entire worlds in each situation and each person encountered. We slow ourselves to be more gentle with these experiences, to take care to let their possibilities, their rich density emerge. We continue moving through time, but we also move into time, allowing it to expand in depth for us though its objective duration diminishes.

Wrinkling—articulation. One of the processes of aging that we recognize most easily is the alteration of smooth surfaces and straight lines, skin wrinkles and roughens; posture becomes curved; memory is restructured; formerly unbroken stretches of clarity are marked by peaks and between them hollows called "confusion." What positive human meaning could such phenomena suggest?

It is as though, through the changes, body and mind express the greater intricacies, the finer articulation that are possible in the person for whom reality has become many-layered, folded upon itself, woven and richly textured, a reality no longer ordered in the more familiar linear fashion, but now a world filled with leaps, windings, countless crossings, immeasurably more intricate and perhaps also more true than the world of one-dimensional thought and self-evident distinctions.

Becoming rigid and flaccid—defining the self. Another process of aging —important because it alters both appearance and movement—is revealed in the phenomenon in which certain parts of the body become rigid and fixed, while others become soft and flaccid. If we think of the skeleton as defining the body's essential form, and the soft tissue as being inessential to structure *per se*, then we see that the final firming occurs in the structurally essential parts, while the tissue that grows flaccid is the structurally inessential. The skeleton settles into a final, rigid form, firm in places where previously mobile, while muscles, for example, grow soft and irrelevant.

Is the body expressing something that we might understand as symbolic for the experience of the person as a whole in aging? Perhaps the hardening is a final structuring, a settling on what one's character and essence are to be, once and for all; and the softening, a dropping away of what one decides is not to be incorporated into the essential structure, the completed character. This does not mean that aging is not a time of growth. It is a growing clearer and more decided about the essence, the form, that one wants one's existence to have, a growing firmer in those features that will be the defining shape of the person.

Relating to one's death. It seems that amid all of the changes and indicators of aging that we see, somewhere death is foreseen. One more meaning of aging thus may be the individual's recognition, conscious or not, that life is finite. The sum of all the changes in aging perhaps indicates a tacit, organic knowledge that death is a reality.

A fatal syndrome has been observed in vigorous, previously healthy persons when told they had cancer; overnight, they became apathetic and withdrawn and within a matter of weeks died, without any satisfactory explanation for death upon autopsy. It may be that aging is the less dramatic form of this self-willed death. We are not suddenly told that we have cancer, but we are told from the beginning that we are mortal, that we will die. Moreover, we need not hear this from the geriatrician, gerontologist, or the philosopher. We need not hear it at all because we tacitly know it with our body and spirit if not our intellect. The patients described above died when told they had a deadly disease. Perhaps aging is the way in which we begin taking account of death when we know, at least implicitly, that life itself, like a fatal illness, is something from which we will die. If one consciously attends to the body's foresight, aging can be used as an opportunity to personally, freely decide what significance the coming death will have for the life that remains. And it is just that freedom, finally, which is the essence of aging as a human value.

Geri Berg lives in Portland, Oregon, where she is a pediatric social worker at Kaiser's Developmental Assessment Clinic. She works with child advocacy groups. Married and the mother of four adult children, she cares for the end-of-life needs of her elderly parents.

Sally Gadow holds nursing degrees from the University of Texas at Galveston and UCSF and a Ph.D. in philosophy from the University of Texas at Austin. She currently teaches nursing at the University of Colorado Health Sciences Center and philosophy at the University of Colorado at Denver. She has edited *Nursing Images and Ideals* and an anthology on the humanities and aging, *What Does it Mean to Grow Old?* Gadow's areas of scholarship include health care ethics, ecology, women's health care, postmodern ethics, and philosophy of health care in correctional settings.

King Lear

Helen M. Luke

CORDELIA;   For thee, oppressed king am I cast down;
                    Myself could else out-frown false fortune's frown—
                    Shall we not see these daughters and these sisters?
LEAR;   No, no, no, no! come let's away to prison:
                    We two alone will sing like birds i'the cage:
                    When thou dost ask me blessing, I'll kneel down
                    And ask of thee forgiveness; so we'll live,
                    And pray, and sing, and tell old tales, and laugh
                    At gilded butterflies, and hear poor rogues
                    Talk of court news, and we'll talk with them too.—
                    Who loses and who wins; who's in, who's out—
                    And take upon's the mystery of things,
                    As if we were God's spies: and we'll wear out,
                    In a wall'd prison, packs and sects of great ones,
                    That ebb and flow by th'moon.

Surely in all the poetry of the world, there could be no more profoundly beautiful, wise, and tender expression of the essence of old age, of the kind of life to which one may come in the last years if one has, like Lear, lived through and accepted all the passion and suffering, the darkness and light, the beauty and horror of one's experience of the world and of oneself.

At a first reading, it is easy to miss the profundity, absorbed as we are in the drama, and see it only as a beautiful fantasy of the old man seeking peace behind actual prison walls with his beloved daughter. But, on a second, third, and fourth reading, who could fail to realize the immensity of the images, and to see how little an actual dungeon has to do with the story?

Cordelia wishes to go out to meet the evil thing and confront it. Because she is young, this response is true and right. For the old, this is no longer the way— "No, no, no, no! Come, let's away to prison." As a man grows old, his body weakens, his powers fail, his sight perhaps is dimmed, his hearing fades, or his power to move around is taken from him. In one way or another, he is "imprisoned," and the moment of choice will come to him. Will he fight this confining process or will he go to meet it in the spirit of King Lear—embrace it with love, with eagerness even? The wisdom of common speech which we so often miss, speaks to us in the phrase, "He is growing old." We use it indiscriminately about those who are being dragged into it, protesting, resisting, crying out against their inevitable imprisonment. Only to one who can say with his or her whole being, "Come, let's away to prison," does this essay apply.

"We two alone will sing like birds i' the cage." We may think of Cordelia in this context as the old man's inner child—the love and courage, the simplicity and innocence of his soul, to which suffering has united him. Cordelia, as Harold C. Goddard has so beautifully pointed out, while remaining an entirely human person, is also a spirit. Throughout the play, she is a symbol of the innocence, the true feeling, that the king so brutally rejected, to which he so blessedly returns, and which, in the instant before death, brings to him, in a flash of vision, the full realization of immortality. So, as the bird pours out notes of joy in its cage, the old man will sing out of his pure love of life in the prison of his enforced inactivity.

Now come those two wonderful lines, "When thou dost ask me blessing, I'll kneel down and ask of thee forgiveness." If an old person does not feel his need to be forgiven by the young, he or she certainly has not grown into age, but merely fallen into it, and his or her "blessing" would be worth nothing. The lines convey with the utmost brevity and power the truth that the blessing that the old may pass on to the young springs only out of that humility that is the fruit of wholeness, the humility that knows *how* to kneel, *how* to ask forgiveness. The old man kneels, not in order to ease guilt feelings (which is at the root of so much apologizing) but in the full and free acceptance of that which Charles Williams called *co-inherence*. King Lear does not say, "I am not worthy to bless you, only to grovel at your feet." He says, "When you ask me blessing, I'll kneel… " The kneeling is the blessing.

"So we'll live," he continues. The exchange of blessings between one human being and another is the essence of life itself. "And pray, and sing, and tell old tales, and laugh at gilded butterflies…" Here are the proper occupations of old age: prayer, which is the quickening of the mind, the rooting of the attention in the ground of being: song, which is the expression of spontaneous joy in the harmony of chaos; the "telling of old tales," which among all primitives was the supreme function of the old, who passed on the wisdom of the ancestor through the symbol, through the understanding of the dreams of the race that their long experience had taught them. In our days how sadly lost, despised even, is the function of the old! Wisdom being identified with knowledge, the "old tale" has become the subject of learned historical research and only for the few does it remain the carrier of true wisdom of heart and mind, of body and spirit. When the old cease to "dream dreams," to be "tellers of old tales," the time must come of which the Book of Proverbs speaks: "Where there is no vision, the people perish."

And laughter! Surely laughter of a certain kind springs from the heart of those who have truly grown old. It is the laughter of pure delight in beauty—beauty of which the golden butterfly is the perfect symbol— a fleeting, ephemeral thing, passing on the wind, eternally reborn from the earth-bound worm, the fragile yet omnipotent beauty of the present moment.

All these four things are activities *without purpose*; any one of them is immediately killed by any hint of striving for achievement. They come to birth only in a heart freed from preoccupation with the goals of the ego, however "spiritual" or lofty these goals may be.

This, however, does not mean that in old age we are to separate ourselves from concern with the world. Without a pause, without even a new sentence, Shakespeare adds to praying, singing, the telling of tales, and laughter an image of listening—listening to the smallest concerns of those still caught in the goals of power. This kind of imprisonment is never a shutting out, a rejection. "And hear poor rogues talk of court news; and we'll talk with them too—who loses and who wins; who's in, who's out." Not only does the wise old man listen, he responds: "and we'll talk with them too." It is not a matter of listening in a superior manner to problems that the king has outgrown. We feel the smiling tenderness of that phrase "poor rogues," untainted by contempt or boredom, and we can almost hear the old king gravely answering each with his own truth, always interested and concerned, never preaching, but offering to each some glimpse of inner freedom.

There follow the few words that are the climax of the whole speech— only a line and a half—words so moving, of such shining beauty, that if they are heard in the depths of one's being, they can surely never be forgotten but will sing in one's heart for the rest of time. "And take upon's the mystery of things, as if we were God's spies." This is the final responsibility of each person's life. Will we or will we not, as we approach the prison of old age, accept this supreme task? It is not the function of the old to explain or to analyze or to impart information. To them comes the great opportunity of taking upon themselves the mystery of things, of becoming, as it were, God's spies. A spy is one who penetrates into a hidden mystery, and a spy of God is that one who sees at the heart of every manifestation of life, even behind the trivial talk of "poor rogues," the *mysterium tremendum* that is God. Explanations and information, necessary as they are along the way, make clear only partial truths, and the danger of mistaking half-truths for truth itself cannot be exaggerated. We are inclined to use the word "mystery" when we are really speaking of a confused muddle or an ignorant superstition. On the contrary, the true mystery is the eternal paradox at the root of life itself—it is that which, instead of hiding truth, reveals the whole, not the part. So, when after having made every effort to understand, we are ready to take upon *ourselves* the mystery of things, then the most trivial of happenings is touched by wonder, and there may come to us, by grace, a moment of unclouded vision.

"And we'll wear out, in a wall'd prison, packs and sects of great ones, that ebb and flow by th'moon." "In a wall'd prison" the spirit of the king is free, while those who think they have made themselves great through the instinctive greed of the pack, through fanatical assertion of the rights of sects or party, are the truly imprisoned. They are the ones at the mercy of the ebb and flow of the unconscious forces they despise. The king himself had been one of these "great ones," driven by his lust for flattery, blind to all individual feeling values, dominated by the ebb and flow of the moon, the unconscious, undifferentiated feminine within. But now, at the end, the storm of his suffering has transmuted the lust and cruelty of the pack, of the mob, into tenderness and compassion, has swept away the blind sectarian judgments of his vanity, leaving him alone, a free individual with his Cordelia, his innocence reborn.

"We'll wear out the packs and sects...." What a cry of hope - more than that - of certainty for the human spirit in this world of totalitarian values! One man alone, embracing his prison, reborn into innocence, can "outwear" their terrifying power, not only through patience and suffering, but through prayer and song and laughter and telling of old tales. The rocket and the bomb can never at the last prevail over the golden butterfly. This was Shakespeare's ultimate certainty. "How with this rage shall beauty hold a plea, whose action is no stronger than a flower? [Sonnet #65]" How indeed? And yet it does, he answers in his greatest plays, notably in the miraculous ending of *King Lear*.

Into these twelve brief lines, spoken by an old man of eighty, Shakespeare has condensed all the essential wisdom into which we may hope to grow in our closing years; but they do not speak only to the very old. At every age, in every person, there comes a partial imprisonment, a disabling psychic wound, an unavoidable combination of circumstances, a weakness that we cannot banish, but must simply accept. Necessity in all its forms imprisons us, and, if we could always with a single heart say to our own "Cordelias," "Come, let's away to prison: we two alone will sing like birds i' the cage," the confining walls would become the alchemist's retort. Inside this retort we would "take upon's the mystery of things," and so the base metal would be transmuted into gold.

How clumsy at the last seem all these words - indeed all words that purport to explain or illuminate great poetry! Yet often we need them to awaken our dulled perception; we speak and hear them so that we may turn from them again and let the poetry itself speak to us out of silence.

No, no, no, no! Come let's away to prison:
We two alone will sing like birds i' the cage.
When thou dost ask me blessing, I'll kneel down
And ask of thee forgiveness; so we'll live,

And pray, and sing, and tell old tales, and laugh
At gilded butterflies, and hear poor rogues
Talk of court news; and we'll talk with them too.—
Who loses and who wins; who's in, who's out;—
And take upon's the mystery of things,
As if we were God's spies; and we'll wear out,
In a wall'd prison, packs and sects of great ones,
That ebb and flow by th'moon.

(Lear V. iii 8–19)

Helen Luke (1904-1995) received a Masters degree in French and Italian literature from Somerville College Oxford before turning to the study of Jungian psychology in Zurich and London. Coming to the United States in 1949, she first worked in Los Angeles as a counselor and later founded the Apple Farm Community near Three Rivers, Michigan. *Old Age*, the essay collection from which "King Lear" is taken, was published in 1987 by Parabola Books.

Suggested Reading

Birtha, Becky. "In the Life." *Lavender Mansions:40 Contemporary Lesbian and Gay Short Stories*, ed. Irene Zahava. Boulder: Westview, 1994.

Blythe, Ronald. *The View in Winter.* New York: Harcourt Brace, 1979.

Cowley, Malcolm. *The View from 80.* New York: Viking, 1980.

Deming, Barbara. "Death and the Old Woman." *Wash Us and Comb Us.* New York: Grossman, 1972.

Grumbach, Doris. *Chamber Music.* New York: Dutton, 1979.

Jolley, Elizabeth. *The Newspaper of Claremont Street.* Freemantle, Western Australia: Freemantle Arts Centre Press, 1985.

Noggle, Anne. *Silver Lining.* Photographs. Text by Janice Zita Grover. Albuquerque, NM: University of New Mexico Press, 1983.

Kohn, Martin et al., eds. *Literature & Aging. An Anthology on Aging.* Kent, OH: Kent State University Press, 1992.

Laurence, Margaret. *The Stone Angel.* Toronto: McClelland and Stewart, 1964.

McCutcheon, Priscilla and Margaret Fowler, eds. *Songs of Experience. An Anthology of Literature on Growing Old.* New York: Ballantine, 1991.

Munro, Alice. "Spelling." *The Beggar Maid.* New York: Random House, 1991.

Olsen, Tillie. *Tell Me a Riddle.* New York: Delacourt/Seymour Lawrence, 1961.

Rule, Jane. *Memory Board.* Tallahassee: Naiad Press, 1987.

Sarton, May. *At 70. A Journal.* New York: Norton, 1984.

Scott-Maxwell, Florida. *The Measure of My Days.* New York: Penguin Books, 1968.

Sennett, Dorothy, ed. *Full Measure. Modern Short Stories on Aging.* St. Paul: Graywolf, 1988.

About the Editor

Margaret Cruikshank has been teaching and writing about women's issues since 1975. She taught English for many years at City College of San Francisco and now teaches women's studies at the University of Maine and occasionally at the University of Southern Maine. Her book *Learning to be Old: gender, culture, and aging,* was published in 2003. She lives in Corea, Maine, a small village on the Gouldsboro Peninsula.